Disclaimer

The information contained in this book is not intended as, and shall not be understood or construed as, financial advice. I am not an attorney, accountant or financial advisor, nor am I holding myself out to be. The information presented in this book is not a substitute for financial advice from a professional who is aware of the facts and circumstances of your individual situation.

I expressly recommend you seek advice from a professional before making any investment decisions.

Cryptocurrencies: Ponzi Schemes, Bubbles and Bitcoin

Copyright © 2021 by Alastair Dorsett

All rights reserved. No parts of this book may be reproduced without written permission except in the form of brief quotations for critical articles and reviews.

Table of Contents

Introduction 7

Chapter 1:
The Ponzi scheme 11
   Charles Ponzi and the original Ponzi scheme 14
   Modern day Ponzi schemes 24
   The biggest Ponzi scheme of the 20th century 24
   Ponzi schemes variations 26
   Multi-level marketing pyramid schemes 27
   Pyramid coaching schemes 30
   What makes Ponzi schemes attractive? 33

Chapter 2:
Currencies and cryptocurrencies 37
   What is a currency? 38
   What is a cryptocurrency? 40
   Why were cryptocurrencies invented? 42

The lifecycle of a cryptocurrency 44

Chapter 3:
Busting cryptocurrency myths 47
Cryptocurrencies are not investments 47
Cryptocurrencies make terrible currencies. 50
Cryptocurrencies can be lost forever 54
Cryptocurrency exchanges 58
Environmental impact 61
Regulation risks 63
Cryptocurrencies are not a store of value. 66
Cryptocurrencies are not commodities. 68
Why decentralised finance doesn't work 69
Cryptocurrencies often fail. 73

Chapter 4:
Crypto, the greatest Ponzi scheme 75
Similarities between crypto and Ponzi schemes 75
Ponzi scheme red flags. 76
Pump and dump schemes. 78
OneCoin Ponzi scheme. 81
Crypto bank Ponzi schemes 86

   Cult-like cultures in crypto now 89

Chapter 5:
How does it all end? 93
   The five stages of a market bubble 94
   The psychology of market bubbles 95
   Tulip mania of the 1630's. 97
   The great depression of the 1930's. 100
   Japans lost decade of 1980's and 1990's 103
   Dot com bubble of the 1990's 105
   Global Financial Crisis 2000's. 108
   The crypto bubble 2020's. 111

Closing thoughts 115

Other books by Alastair Dorsett. 117

About the author 118

*"I went looking for **trouble**, and I found it"*

Charles Ponzi

Introduction

Did you know that as of January 2021, there were over 4000 cryptocurrencies in existence and that 40% of those have failed? And did you know that most cryptocurrencies share many characteristics of Ponzi schemes?

What about the fact that the cryptocurrency market is showing all the classic signs of being in a speculative bubble?

Are you still considering that "once in a lifetime" cryptocurrency investment? Have you heard people singing the praises of cryptocurrencies and the stellar returns they are making on some new cryptocurrency that is definitely going to change the world? Or maybe you are just wondering what all the fuss is about and is this technology really as good as everyone is saying?

Whether you have already invested in cryptocurrencies or you are thinking about it, you should know what the world of cryptocurrencies is really like beneath the bright lights of social media hype. There are countless cryptocurrency trading gurus just waiting to sell you the dream of getting rich quick but the world of cryptocurrencies has a dark side to it that cryptocurrency advocates don't tell you about.

The world of cryptocurrencies is full of con men, Ponzi schemes, speculative bubbles and outright fraud. The risks involved with investing your money into cryptocurrencies is hard to overstate. The picture painted on social media and online is just a small part of the real world that exists beneath the shiny marketing material and enthusiastic hype.

You only hear about the few people that have made great returns investing in cryptocurrencies but have you ever heard from the thousands that have lost money investing in cryptocurrencies? The chances are, you haven't.

When it comes to falling victim to scams or poor investment choices, a vast majority of people do not report it or tell others about it. Often feelings of shame are the reason. Most of us would not want others to think less of them for falling victim to what in hindsight, is obviously as scam. There is a certain shame people feel when faced with the fact they have been taken for a ride that stops them from advertising it to others.

Think about it, when was the last time you saw someone post a picture on social media of a losing bet they made? I doubt you'll be able to think of a single example. On the other hand, how many people shout about the winning bet they made? The chances are you've seen a few example of this. Good and bad investments are the same. People tend to shout about the winners and never the losers, the result is a skewed perception of the risks involved.

When it comes to the world of cryptocurrencies, the winners and the people at the top of the pyramid shout the loudest and post all over social media, attracting mass attention and hype, pulling in more investors. Fearing they'll miss out on the next big thing, some investors blindly put their money into the next new cryptocurrency with very little due diligence or research on what they are giving their money to. Needless to say, it often ends badly.

But you don't hear about those failures very often because the Facebook friend that posted about a once in a lifetime investment, isn't then going to come and admit that they had lost all their money. This culture of only showing the positives has allowed the industry to proliferate and grow to the size it is today.

Even though cryptocurrencies are a relatively recent phenomenon, what many don't realise is that these kinds of investment patterns and schemes are nothing new. The only things that change are the people and the investment product. We can look to history and learn from investment scams of the past, look at their characteristics and see if there are similarities to any new investment opportunities that come along such as cryptocurrencies.

Do you know how to tell if a cryptocurrency you are presented with is a Ponzi scheme for example? How would you know? What is a Ponzi scheme , how do you spot one and why are they bad? You might think that regulators in your country will be able to protect you from falling victim to these schemes but no. These schemes continue to spread and grow right up to this day in all manner of guises. Spotting a Ponzi scheme is an easy to learn skill that every investor needs to know in a world where they are so common.

When you compare the recent spikes in cryptocurrency market caps to other bubbles throughout history, the pattern is clear to see. It all points to the cryptocurrency market experiencing a huge speculative bubble. Individual cryptocurrencies are often subject to extreme volatility where prices are inflated quickly before crashing. Again, how would you spot whether this is happening? What would you look for? This is also an area where we can look to the past for advice. There have been many speculative bubbles over the centuries and the same characteristics mark every market bubble since the first recorded market bubble in the 1600's.

With every speculative bubble in the past, there were people who said that a bubble did not exist and that another crash was impossible. There is always someone that claims the market will keep rising and never fall. Yet crashes happen every time speculation runs rife. Every bubble pops just as every Ponzi scheme fails. With both speculative bubbles and Ponzi schemes, failure isn't a question of if, it's a question of when. How many investors will get caught out is hard to say, the aim is to make sure you aren't one of them.

The nefarious and shady world of cryptocurrency investing will be revealed for what it is in the coming chapters. Ponzi schemes will be exposed, market bubbles will be popped and all the promises of getting rich quick on cryptocurrencies will be torn apart.

Chapter 1:

The Ponzi scheme

The term Ponzi scheme is just another name for a pyramid scheme. There are a few different variations of pyramid scheme but they all follow the same basic formula. A pyramid scheme is a fraudulent investment opportunity where investors are paid a return on their original investment using the cash from investors who came after them. This model is also referred to as "robbing Peter to pay Paul". This type of scheme will always have less capital than what they owe because of this. The schemes will work as long as new investors keep joining with cash to pay old investors. Inevitably with no actual growth of the capital or value creation, they always fail.

Sometimes schemes can run for years before failing and so the fact that a scheme has been running for a number of years, does not mean it is legitimate. Some of the most notorious Ponzi schemes in history ran for over 20 years before collapsing. The reason Ponzi schemes always fail is down to simple mathematics. Ponzi schemes have to continue to grow exponentially in order for every new investor to get paid. This is impossible as there are a finite number of people on earth. Every Ponzi scheme is bound by this limit. There are a finite number of investors available that will sign up and when they run out, which they will because their number is finite, the Ponzi scheme will no longer be able to sustain its pay-outs and it will fail.

The diagram below demonstrates this point. The top of the

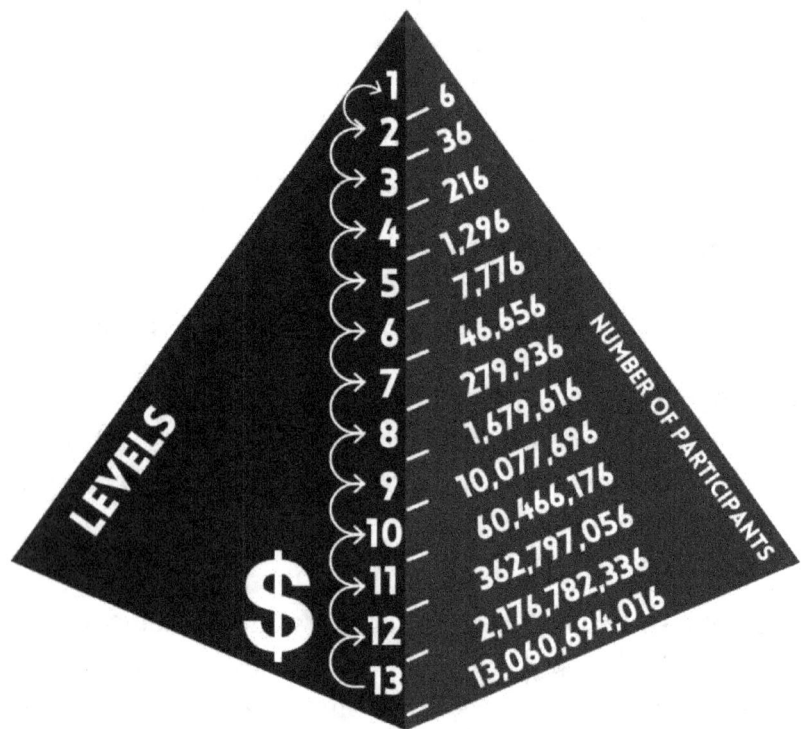

pyramid represents early investors or the people who run the scheme, money moves from the lower levels of the pyramid towards the top.

In the diagram, for each investor to get paid their returns, 6 new investors have to join the scheme. So in this example, for the 6 investors at the top level of the pyramid to get paid, 36 new investors need to join at the second level in the pyramid. For those 36 new investors to get paid at level 2, 216 new investors have to join at level 3. For those 216 investors to get paid at level 3, 1,296 investors have to join at level 4 and so on. After just 13 levels, more than 13 billion people would have to join for the people at level 12 to get paid. There are only about 7 billion people on planet earth. For this Ponzi scheme example to carry on, more people than the total number of people on earth would have to join. As you can see due to the finite number of people of earth, the failure of a Ponzi scheme is always assured.

The failure of a Ponzi scheme often comes about rapidly and out of the blue. Usually a small, seemingly insignificant event triggers the collapse, which takes investors by surprise. Usually it starts when new investment eventually starts drying up. Current investors stop getting paid or restrictions start being set on withdrawals from the scheme. Reality starts setting in for previously enthusiastic investors. Word spreads and panic spread with it. Investors demand their money and when the scheme cannot pay out, only then do they discover that the scheme does not have enough money to pay back all the deposits that were made. The scheme then collapses and investors often lose most of their investment.

In the wake of a Ponzi scheme collapse, it usually all comes out how the scheme operated. It is usually as simple as all the funds being deposited and paid from a single bank account. The people running the scheme will usually have skimmed lots of fees and commission out of the fund to pay for a lavish lifestyle whilst the scheme is running.

In the past, it was usually these people that get caught and jailed for fraud. In the modern era however, with the advent of the internet, Ponzi schemes can now be run anonymously which allows the culprits to disappear with the remains of investors' funds when the scheme fails. These fraudsters are then free to set up another scheme and repeat the cycle again.

Charles Ponzi and the original Ponzi scheme

There have been many notable Ponzi schemes over the past 150 or so years but the Ponzi scheme takes its name from a notorious Italian swindler, Charles Ponzi born in 1882. Ponzi was an interesting character and we can learn a lot about pyramid schemes from Ponzi's story, his original scheme and how he pulled it off.

It is said Ponzi came from an upper class family that had fallen on hard times. Ponzi's first job was as a postal worker before he was accepted into the University of Rome La Sapienza.

At university, the people he became friends with generally came from upper class families and they considered university a four year vacation. Ponzi, coming from a family that had in the recent past been an upper class family, had a similar mind-set to his friends. He attempted to emulate the party lifestyle of his rich friends even though his family was no longer rich and could not support this lifestyle the way his friends families could. He predictably ended up broke after four years and without a degree.

One thing he did leave University with was an appetite for a lavish lifestyle. It is also likely that at University he developed his charm and charisma that would allow him to become such successful swindler later in life.

After his time in Rome, his family, seeing other young Italian men immigrating to America and returning wealthy, encouraged Ponzi to do the same. They wanted him to travel to America, make it big and restore his family to its former glory. In 1903, at the age of 21, Ponzi boarded a ship and travelled to America. Ponzi got on the ship with all of his remaining savings but on the journey, his tendency to live above his means got the better of him. He arrived in Boston with $2.50 to his name after gambling the rest of his savings on the journey over. Already at the age of 21 he had bankrupted himself twice trying to live a lifestyle he couldn't sustain. This was a pattern that looked set to continue.

Once in America, Ponzi as resourceful as he was, quickly learned English and took to doing odd jobs along the East Coast before taking a job as a dishwasher in a restaurant. Ponzi had to sleep on the floor in the restaurant as he was so poor. Ponzi soon managed to work his way up to a waiter position at the restaurant. However, his appetite for a luxury lifestyle had not left him. The modest salary of a waiter was not good enough, he wanted more and he wanted it fast. He first showed his criminal tendencies in this job when he was fired for theft and for short changing customers. It wouldn't be long before he was short changing customers on a much larger scale.

Having failed to become successful in America, Ponzi moved to Montreal where he used his charismatic personality and ability to speak English, Italian and French to land a job as a clerk in a bank called Banco Zarossi. It was at Banco Zarossi that Ponzi was first introduced to the pyramid scheme or "robbing Peter to pay Paul" as some would put it. The bank promised customers a return of 6% on their deposits which was double the going rate at the time and became incredibly popular as a result.

When Ponzi eventually rose to the position of bank manager, it seemed as if he had finally found an honest living he was good at and one that paid more than a modest waiter's salary. This wasn't to last long. He soon discovered how the bank was able to pay such high interest rates. The bank wasn't using profits from its investments to pay these high interest rates, it was using the money deposited in newly opened accounts to pay these interest rates. The bank was operating a pyramid scheme and as we know, pyramid schemes always fail.

The bank inevitably fell into serious financial trouble as a result of the pyramid scheme it was running. The troubles were compounded by a series of bad real estate loans the bank had made. Predictably, the bank eventually failed and once again, Ponzi was left penniless. The owner fled to Mexico with a large proportion of the banks remaining money, some of which was Ponzi's own money he had earned from his job as the banks manager.

Down on his luck again, Ponzi decided he would return to the US. Whilst planning his return to the US, Ponzi made his next criminal mistake. He walked into the offices of a former Banco Zarossi customer and finding no one there, helped himself to a cheque from a cheque book left in the office. Ever the opportunist, he wrote himself a cheque for a large sum of money and forged the owner's signature. Ponzi was caught soon after the cheque was cashed and after admitting to his crime, was sentenced to three years in prison.

Ponzi was released from prison in 1911 at the age of 29. He returned to America once again soon after his release. However, his freedom wouldn't last. Trouble never seemed to escape Ponzi for too long. He found himself back in jail for another two years when he got involved in a scheme to smuggle illegal Italian immigrants across the border between Canada and America.

After he was released from prison once again, he returned to Boston. Over the next few years he once again drifted between jobs around Boston and in 1918 he married. Shortly after, he worked at his father in laws grocery store then an import-export company before he started his own advertising business. His business soon failed and when it did, he took over his wife's family's fledgling fruit company. This company didn't last long before it failed under his leadership. Already, Ponzi had shown he was unable to hold down a job and had a track record for failed businesses under his leadership.

It was in the summer of 1919 that the idea for the original "Ponzi scheme" came to Charles Ponzi. He had received a letter from a company in Spain inquiring about his advertising company. In the envelope, an International Reply Coupon (IRC) was included. Ponzi had never heard of these before.

The purpose of an IRC was to allow someone in one country to send a letter to someone in another country and also pay for their reply. An IRC allowed the person receiving the letter to exchange the IRC for stamps to cover the cost of postage in whichever country the IRC was redeemed. The IRCs were priced at the cost of postage in the country in which they were bought and could be exchanged for stamps to cover the cost of postage in the country they were redeemed. If these values were different, a profit could be made.

Inflation in Italy after World War One meant that postage costs in Italy when expressed in US dollars had decreased substantially. This allowed a person to purchase cheap IRCs in Italy and then exchange them for US stamps of a higher value. Ponzi worked out that at the time, the profit from such a transaction could be in excess of 400%. This method of making profit is called arbitrage. The fundamental idea behind it is to buy an asset in one market and then immediately sell it in another market for a higher price. It is simply the practise of taking advantage of inefficient pricing between different markets. It was (and still is) perfectly legal. So how did it all go wrong?

Seeing an opportunity, Ponzi quit his job and went about setting up his IRC scheme. To make the largest profit margins, Ponzi needed to raise capital to buy IRCs in the cheap European market. He initially tried to borrow money from banks but was turned down when he couldn't convince them of the merits of his scheme. Ponzi's criminal background and track record for failed business ventures probably didn't help his case. You could say this was the first warning flag for his scheme; banks wouldn't touch it.

Ponzi persevered and eventually listed a company called the Securities Exchange Company to sell shares and raise money from the general public. He also went to his friends and promised 50% returns in only 45 days (remember, interest rates at this time were 5% annually). Tempted by the stellar returns promised, some of these people invested early and were paid back as promised. Pleased with their incredible returns, they spread word of Ponzi's investment opportunity.

It wasn't long before investors started coming to Ponzi to invest in his IRC scheme. Ponzi made his scheme seem more exclusive than it was and made investors feel as if he was letting them into something exclusive that wasn't available to ordinary investors. Ponzi paid his early investors with the money received from new investors. As these early investors were paid promptly and as promised, they spread the word further to family and friends. When people saw how well their trusted family or friend had done with their investment, many would also throw money at Ponzi's scheme.

As his scheme gained popularity, Ponzi expanded his offices and hired agents to promote his scheme further afield. A fear of missing out on this golden opportunity whipped up a buying frenzy. A lot of investors instead of taking profits were now also reinvesting in the scheme. Some were re-mortgaging their homes and investing their life savings. Ponzi was soon making millions per day and even took up a controlling interest in a bank, further increasing his credibility.

This was all ultimately doomed to come crashing down. The simplest financial analysis that any investor could do would show that Ponzi's scheme was running at a loss and simply relied upon more and more new investors depositing money into the scheme. If someone had bothered to think about it logically, they would have seen that stamps could not easily or quickly be exchanged for cash in large numbers.

The big challenge would have been physically selling the sheer numbers of stamps that would be required to pay these investors. After all, who would buy millions of dollars' worth of stamps at once? No one would and so they would have to be sold individually or in small batches. It would be as good as impossible to actually sell the volume of stamps required to cover the returns paid by the scheme.

Applying this logic, they would have seen that for an initial investment of $1800, it would have taken 53,000 IRCs to realise the arbitrage profits. That doesn't even take into account the difficulty of selling the stamps the 53,000 IRCs would be converted to. If you scaled this up to the millions of dollars per day flooding into the scheme, you would see that you would have to fill titanic sized ships with IRCs and ship them to America. You would then have to exchange them for stamps and then sell the stamps. A logistical impossibility.

Ponzi realised this early on but found that as long as new investment was flooding in, his scheme could stay afloat. Ponzi was soon living the lifestyle he had always wanted. He was living in luxury on the money flooding into the scheme. He bought houses, cars and even bought a few small companies, including a controlling stake in a bank in the hope that the profits from these companies could be used to sustain the IRC scheme.

The rise of the scheme naturally drew suspicion. Any public accusations were quickly put down by Ponzi. When a financial writer suggested that there was no way Ponzi could legally deliver the profits promised, Ponzi sued him for libel. He won $500,000 in damages, an incredible amount at the time. Libel law at the time required the writer or publisher to prove their claims and so without proof, no serious probes into the scheme took place lest they also get sued for libel.

Eventually the Boston Post published a series of articles asking questions of Ponzi's scheme. The articles noted that Ponzi himself did not invest his money in his own scheme. It was also then noted that in order to cover the investments within Ponzi's scheme, 160 million IRCs would have to be in circulation. In reality, only 27,000 were in circulation and according to the US post office, IRCs were not being bought in quantity. The articles also claimed that the overheads involved in handling the purchase and redemption of so many IRCs would exceed any potential profit you could make.

This series of articles caused a panic run on the Securities Exchange Company where droves of investors crowded outside its offices demanding their money back. Ponzi used his charisma and charm to calm the crowd and began paying investors back their money. After three days and a couple of million dollars paid out, many investors' nerves were settled and many no longer demanded their money back.

However, the writing was on the wall for Ponzi. His publicist discovered incriminating documents detailing how the scheme wasn't actually profitable and relied solely on new investor's cash to pay old investors. His publicist then sold the story to the Boston Post who published it causing another frenzied run on the Securities Exchange Company.

Now Ponzi was using loans from the bank he had a controlling interest of to prop up his company and pay investors. When bank examiners ordered the bank to stop lending Ponzi money, it all came crashing down. An audit revealed Ponzi was $7 million in debt and soon after, his criminal past was exposed in the Boston Post. He was soon arrested and charged with larceny and mail fraud. He ended up in jail until his release and deportation in 1934.

Ponzi was soon divorced and ended up living in Brazil where his health deteriorated.

He had a heart attack which left him weakened, he was left almost completely blind and a brain haemorrhage left him partially paralysed on one side of his body. He died penniless in 1949 in a charity hospital in Rio de Janeiro. A far cry from the millionaire lifestyle he had enjoyed earlier in life.

It was estimated that investors had lost about $20 million (around $200 million in today's money) through his company. Many investors only ended up getting back 30% of their investment, losing 70% instead of the 50% gain every 45 days they had been promised.

Despite losing almost all of their investments, Ponzi being jailed and piles of evidence that he had scammed them, some people still wanted to put their trust him. Ponzi had been so good at fooling investors that some sent him Christmas cards in jail. Some would even ask him to invest their money again they had so much trust in him. It just goes to show how charismatic Ponzi must have been and it serves as a warning to others to never blindly put their faith in anyone when it comes to investing money.

The ease with which Ponzi's scheme was also proven to be fraudulent is also a lesson we can apply to similar schemes today. One easy way of assessing whether something is a Ponzi scheme is find out where the cash flow for the scheme is coming from. If the only cash flow the scheme generates is from other investors, it is a Ponzi scheme. If money comes from cash flow generating assets, it will more likely be legitimate.

Modern day Ponzi schemes

Despite the notoriety of Ponzi's scheme, many schemes have come and gone since then and many are still going today. Some of the biggest Ponzi schemes in history to be uncovered have happened in the last 20 years or so.

The biggest Ponzi scheme of the 20th century

The biggest Ponzi scheme of the 20th century was executed by Bernie Madoff in the 90's and early 2000's. Bernie Madoff was a popular and trusted figure in the financial industry. He was the chairman of the Nasdaq Composite index for three years and had a good relationship with the regulatory body in the US. Over a period of 17 years he defrauded thousands of investors out of tens of billions of dollars.

He ran a securities firm which claimed to generate large, steady returns using a legitimate but complex investing strategy. In reality, he simply deposited his clients funds into a bank account at Chase Manhattan Bank that he then used to pay people who wanted to cash out. The bank (now called JP Morgan Chase) was estimated to have made around $500 million from these deposits over the years and so was inclined not to look to deeply into these deposits.

He continually attracted new investors and capital in order to fund any clients cashing out. He took a leaf out of Ponzi's book and made his fund seem exclusive to investors to bring them in and keep them in. He also took advantage of his impeccable reputation to gain investors trust and keep them coming to his scheme.

When the 2008 financial crisis hit, investors in general were hit hard. A lot of investors were losing money in the markets and a lot started liquidating their investments to keep themselves afloat. With capital drying up, Madoff was soon unable to attract new investors to cover the investors cashing out. His scheme was collapsing and he confessed his fraud to his sons who turned him in the next day. He was eventually jailed for 150 years. It was later estimated that Madoff had defrauded investors of between $17 billion and $60 billion dollars making it by far the largest Ponzi scheme in history at the time.

Looking back, it seems fairly obvious that Bernie Madoff was up to no good. In 2008 when the S&P 500 dropped 39%, Bernie Madoffs firm reported returns of 5.6%. Looking at those figures alone, it seems obvious now. How could he possibly have been beating the wider market by 45%? It is unheard of and it wouldn't have taken much for any ordinary investor to simply compare the returns Madoff was telling them he was getting and the returns that everyone else in the market was getting. If more had done so, they might have been able to avoid losing their money.

Several analysts in the investing world did flag concerns about Madoffs firm to the Securities Exchange Commission

(SEC) over the years. An analyst uncovered the fraud as early as 2000 when he was tasked to replicate Bernie Madoffs investment strategy for his own firm. When he tried to replicate Madoffs strategy, he discovered very quickly that Madoff was lying. He later said he knew within 5 minutes that Madoffs numbers didn't add up and within four hours, he proved that his returns could only be obtained by fraud. This was all reported to the SEC who then took no action.

You might think that Ponzi schemes would be extremely hard or impossible to operate nowadays given the stringent regulation of the financial industry. In reality, Bernie Madoff showed that they can still operate in plain sight over long periods of time and take billions from investors. Regulatory bodies aren't perfect and investors shouldn't rely solely on them to weed out every bad investment. As regulations evolve to catch these schemes and stop them, the schemes adapt to avoid the regulations. Inevitably, some Ponzi schemes slip through the cracks and do still operate. Investors should therefore apply their own due diligence when investing in anything.

Ponzi schemes variations

There are many examples of Ponzi schemes operating today that are actually legal but still take billions from investors every year. The sad reality is that talking about these types of schemes is often controversial and people often get upset when these schemes are called Ponzi schemes. This is usually because these very people have been caught up in one of these schemes and don't want to believe that they have fallen victim to one.

Multi-level marketing pyramid schemes

One of the most widespread Ponzi schemes still operating all over the world today is the multi-level marketing scheme. There are countless multi-level marketing scheme variations but they all have one thing in common; they are just variations of the original Ponzi scheme. I can almost guarantee that every person reading this will know someone involved in one of these schemes and that there will even be a few reading this that have been involved in this type of scheme. There will be people in your neighbourhood involved with one right now. Think of the post on social media you have seen of a neighbour, family member or friend selling perfume or cosmetics for example. They might also have posted about how they are earning massive amounts working from home and in a short period of time, have risen through several promotions and now have a fancy, important sounding job title. They then go on to say that you can do it too and in doing so try to recruit their friends or family to join the scheme too and earn similar money. You might not have realised it, but schemes like that are just Ponzi schemes.

These types of schemes usually involve recruiting people to work for you selling some sort of product, often beauty products like cosmetics or perfume. This is what makes multi-level marketing schemes legal; their product. The diagram below shows the structure of a multi-level marketing scheme, the majority of the money comes from lower levels in the pyramid up to the higher levels but some money also comes in at all levels from the schemes product.

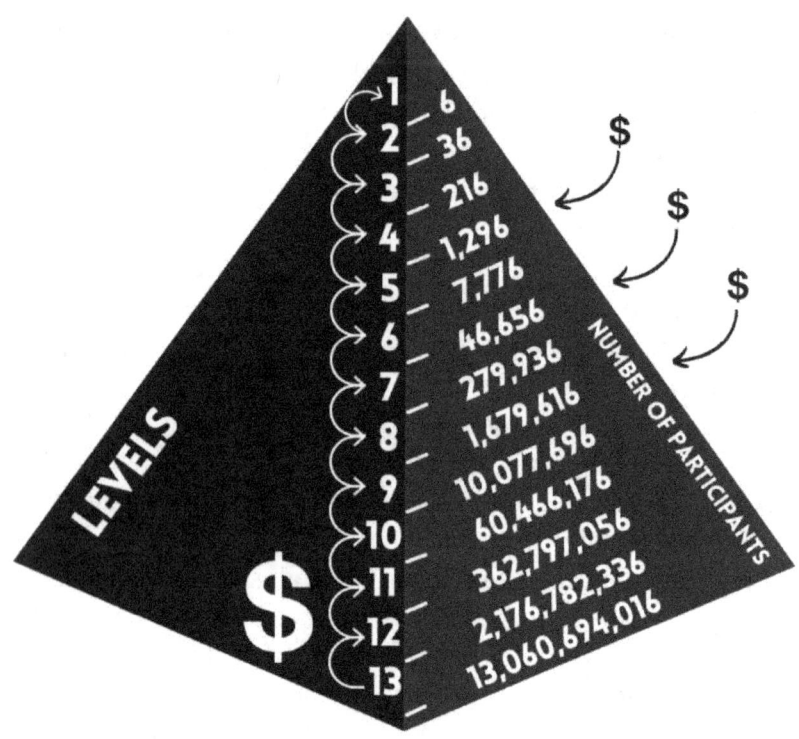

The investor pays to join the scheme and in return is given products to sell. This investor can either make profit by selling these products or by recruiting others into the scheme to sell the products for which they will get a cut of the commission. In reality, the emphasis is on recruiting other investors to the scheme to gain commission on their joining fees who then are in the same position of needing to recruit people to the scheme to make commission. Sounds familiar right? The only thing that keeps these schemes legal is that the people who run them will argue they are selling a product for a profit and not simply recruiting naïve investors to a Ponzi scheme. In most of these schemes, recruiting more people to the scheme is where a majority of the schemes income comes from. When joining, there is usually minimal emphasis on selling their product and instead the emphasis is on recruiting more people to the scheme.

Another familiar hallmark of these schemes is the high returns they promise investors and the abuse of personal, trusted relationships to recruit investors to the scheme. Again, one of the most damaging aspects of Ponzi schemes isn't just the money the investor loses themselves but also the money they encouraged other people to lose. Some studies estimate that over 99.25% of people participating in multi-level marketing schemes didn't make a significant profit and in fact the majority operated at a net loss.

The existence of legal Ponzi schemes in plain sight again reinforces the fact that as investors, it is incredibly dangerous to believe that you are safe from Ponzi schemes or that you'll be able to spot them easily. Trusting an investment opportunity because of its large scale or because your friends or family have invested in it is clearly a dangerous situation too. A lot of the time when friends or family have invested in this type of scheme, it will be incredibly hard to convince them that they are participating in a Ponzi scheme. It can be a hard subject to talk about and allows the schemes to spread further and become more damaging as people do not want to have a difficult conversation with their friends or family.

As we've seen, even the regulators have trouble spotting Ponzi schemes when they're in plain sight and some kinds are not even illegal. The chances are you know someone who has participated in a Ponzi scheme and they may not even know it was a Ponzi scheme.

Pyramid coaching schemes

Another type of pyramid scheme that is becoming increasingly common is the pyramid coaching scheme. This industry is completely unregulated which motivates and captures people with the promise of easy money and a new lifestyle in a similar way to multi-level marketing schemes,

Essentially these schemes involve people with little to no professional qualifications or experience coaching people in how to make money coaching. Where coaching schemes differ fundamentally from other Ponzi schemes is that instead of paying money for the promise of money, you pay money for knowledge that they promise will make you money.

In the diagram below, again the structure is very similar to Ponzi and multi-level marketing schemes. Money flows from the lower levels of the pyramid up to the higher levels but in the case of the pyramid coaching scheme, "coaching" or "knowledge" of some sort flows down.

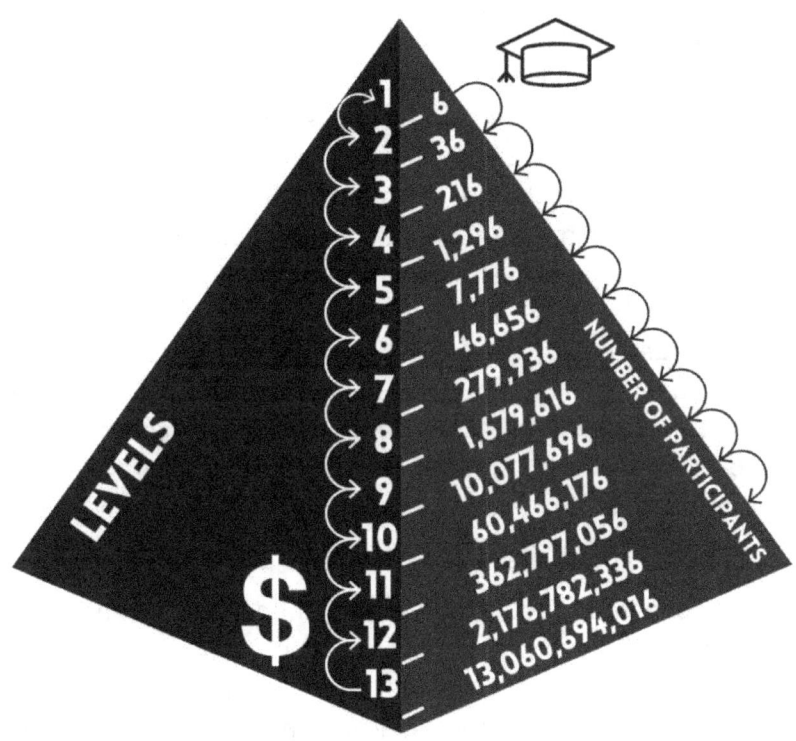

The goal of these schemes is to subscribe people to the scheme, coach them in how to coach with the aim that they will then go out and subscribe more people to the scheme and repeat the cycle. They often try to sell clients progressively more expensive programs, making people believe that the next program will help them to "make it". As with all pyramid schemes, the schemes rely on gaining more subscribers in order to keep the schemes paying out.

As with all Ponzi schemes, the greater fool theory comes into play here. Each coach is relying on finding a greater fool that will pay for their coaching programs in the belief that they will also be able to find someone to sell their coaching programs to and so on. Commonly these schemes are for health coaches, life coaches, businesses coaches, drop shipping coaches and of course cryptocurrency trading coaches. The health coaches will have no medical background or training, life coaches will have no therapist qualifications, business coaches will never have run a successful business, drop shipping coaches will have no unique ideas or products and cryptocurrency coaches will have had no financial experience or qualifications. These are just examples but the idea is that these coaches are people who are completely unqualified and lacking the experience to teach anyone about the subject they are attempting to teach.

These schemes proliferate easily online and often these schemes use tactics such as focussing on the money they say the person signing up will make and give no detail on how they'll get there. Tag lines such as "earn 5 or 6 figures per year from home" and "you can be making money now. Guaranteed!" are common and draw people in with the promise of making easy money. As with most pyramid schemes, most often they are spread through word of mouth and by smooth talking, likeable characters who are great salesmen. Often these schemes end up damaging not just the people who sign up to them, but the people close to those who sign up as they are roped into paying for worthless coaching programs.

With the increasing prevalence of these types of schemes, I'm certain you will know someone personally who has fallen victim to one of these schemes. One easy way of stopping yourself from falling foul of these coaching schemes is to simply adopt this simple rule: If they haven't been there, don't ask them for directions. Meaning if they don't have significant experience or qualifications in the subject they're coaching, then the chances are, they don't know what they're talking about and most likely, their scheme will be a fraud.

What makes Ponzi schemes attractive?

How does common sense evade the thousands of investors who throw their life savings at Ponzi schemes? There are a number of reasons pyramid schemes can be so attractive to people. The promise of spectacular returns in a short time frame speaks to the fundamental greed built into us as humans. The prospect of getting rich quick with little to no effort is a major draw and often makes people disregard the risk involved or fail to recognise the risk altogether. The chances are you've experienced this first hand to some degree. For example, how much more attractive does buying a lottery ticket seem when the jackpot has "rolled over" a few times? You know the chances of you winning are exactly the same; practically zero but the prospect of a higher jackpot than the usual makes buying a ticket seem like a much better idea. Both the Charles Ponzi and Bernie Madoffs schemes demonstrated this perfectly. The prospect of getting rich quick drew thousands to invest in their schemes without asking any questions.

Pyramid schemes are often promoted by charismatic, likeable figures who gain you trust using their great personality and the fantastic deal they're offering. We don't think that people we like would rip us off. In reality, a likeable, charismatic person is the only type of person that will be able to rip you off. You're not going to entrust your hard earned cash to someone you don't like are you? In Ponzi's case, he was often described as charismatic and likable right up until his death. These qualities he used to great effect when promoting his scheme and getting investors to trust him. The fact that even after Ponzi was jailed and investors lost most of their money, some still wrote to him and send him Christmas cards shows just how charismatic and likeable he was. In Bernie Madoffs case, he was an authority figure in the financial industry. He was trusted, he was well known and he held positions of trust and responsibility. He used this to great effect when recruiting investors to his scheme.

Possibly the biggest influencing factor in clouding our judgment when it comes to pyramid schemes is the concept of "social proof". Social proof can be described as the tendency of large groups to conform to a set of behaviours. The underlying assumption is that when we see large numbers of people acting a certain way, we believe that they must possess more information or understanding than us and so we copy that behaviour. This manifests in a pyramid scheme when people invest money based on what friends and family have invested in. They see the gains others have made and assume that they can do the same by copying what they have done without applying any common sense or due diligence. This effect was obvious in both Ponzi's scheme and Madoffs scheme where they grew primarily through word of mouth. This made the schemes all the more damaging as people would have often recommended the investments to their friends or family, destroying trust and relationships when the investments failed and they lost everything.

We all love to trust "expert" opinion when making decisions. Following the opinion of an expert takes the effort away from making a decision for us. We trust that experts in their fields are honest and cannot be corrupted. We often don't check whether an expert is in fact, an expert. When was the last time you verified an "experts" credentials or experience before believing their opinion? The fact is that anyone can claim to be an expert with zero experience or knowledge. The responsibility lies with us to be able to sort through the fake opinions to ones that are actually well informed and considered. Remember that Bernie Madoff was the Chairman of the NASDAQ, a position of tremendous trust and authority. Most investors would trust the integrity and word of a person in such a position when in reality, people in these positions are not always as honest as we would like to think they are.

Chapter 2:

Currencies and cryptocurrencies

The narrative around cryptocurrencies has changed over the years from being intended as a currency to being a store of value. This is simply a convenient way of cryptocurrency advocates attempting to justify cryptocurrencies being utterly terrible and unworkable as currencies. To understand why, we need to look at what currencies and cryptocurrencies are at a fundamental level.

If we are also to draw any links between Ponzi schemes and cryptocurrencies, it also helps to consider what currencies and cryptocurrencies fundamentally are, their purposes, their histories and their usability. If you understand how these things came to be invented and what problems they were trying to solve, you will see how cryptocurrencies have strayed far from their initial design intent.

What is a currency?

Currencies have been used in some form for thousands of years. The fundamental purpose of a currency is simply to facilitate trade. Where currencies don't exist, trades can only happen by bartering goods and services for goods and services. This method of trade is difficult and inefficient. Imagine paying for your weekly shop using bags of grain, a goat or some other commodity. It would be extremely difficult both in terms of transporting and storing these goods but also in agreeing a value for them between you and the other trading party. The other issue with bartering is that some goods are not divisible. If all you have to trade is a goat for example, you cannot buy something of lesser value than a goat as you cannot divide the goat. This is why currencies were invented. They are widely accepted, divisible, there is consensus on their value and they are easy to transport and store.

For thousands of years, most currencies were commodity currencies that took the form of coins often made from precious metals such as gold and silver. The value of these commodity currencies lay in the value of the actual precious metals the coins were made from. This still presented the problem that large amounts could be hard to transport and store.

To solve this, representative currencies were invented. Banks could store commodities, usually gold, in their vault and then issue bank notes representing the value of that gold. These notes allowed the holder in principle to freely exchange their notes for gold and vice versa. Representative currencies allowed money to be even more portable and also made it more divisible. Currencies that operated in this are often referred to as "gold standard" currencies. This doesn't imply they are better, it simply means they are backed by gold.

In the first half of the 20th century, countries started abandoning the gold standard in favour of fiat currencies. Fiat currencies are government issued currencies that are not backed up by any physical commodity such as gold. The value of fiat currencies is maintained by the government issuing them. The governments that issue fiat currencies demand their taxes are paid in these currencies. Because everyone has to pay taxes, people accept the currency in exchange for goods and services.

Fiat currencies have taken over in the modern world because economists argue that gold standard currencies restrict economic growth. Because a finite amount of gold exists, the amount of gold standard currency that can be in circulation is fixed. A restricted supply of money during times of increased productivity acts as a constraint to growth and businesses will struggle to access capital.

The main argument for abandoning the gold standard in favour of fiat currencies is that with fiat currencies, central banks and governments can influence their economies with their monetary policies. Economists believe that increasing the supply of money can stabilize economies and mitigate against recessions. Economists argue that "gold standard" currencies prolonged The Great Depression in countries that were slow to abandon it. Abandoning the gold standard allowed countries to stimulate their economies and helped them rise out of The Great Depression. The importance of being able to control the supply of money is hard to overstate. Despite the commonly held belief that "printing money" or increasing the money supply is always bad, in reality it actually helps modern economies avoid prolonged and deep depressions like The Great Depression.

This could be seen across the world during the 2020 pandemic. Almost a fifth of all US dollars now in existence were "printed" during the 2020 pandemic. The purpose of this policy was to keep economies afloat during the pandemic. The long term effect of such polices are yet to be confirmed. Some argue that the vastly increased money supply will lead to hyperinflation as has been seen in the past in places like 1930's Germany. Others argue that hyperinflation is not the result of money printing but the result of the breakdown of productivity in an economy or because of political instability. So the chances are that as long as countries can keep producing goods and services and their government remains stable, hyperinflation is not a real possibility and could in fact just be scaremongering.

What is a cryptocurrency?

Cryptocurrencies are cryptographically secure digital "assets" touted to work as a method of transferring value in a similar way to regular currencies. Where cryptocurrencies differ is that they are not managed by a central entity such as a central bank or government. Instead they are said to be "decentralised". With a cryptocurrency, transactions are recorded on a distributed public "ledger". This ledger is kept up to date by a distributed network of computers who are referred to as "miners". Miners are rewarded for updating the ledger through the issuance of new currency. The rate at which new cryptocurrency is created is defined at the conception of the currency. The production of new tokens is often designed to be finite and also to reduce with time. This guarantees that there is a cap on the total amount of the currency that will ever be in circulation.

The technology that enabled all this to happen is called blockchain. Blockchain was first described in 1991 but it wasn't until Bitcoin came along in 2008 that blockchain had its first real world use case. The term blockchain comes from the fact that the ledger is made up of many records or "blocks" linked by a "chain" of cryptography.

Cryptography is nothing new, without it, most of the everyday things you do on the internet could not happen. Cryptography is simply the science of keeping information secret and secure by transforming it into a form only the intended recipient can understand. Almost everything you do on the internet nowadays will use cryptography to secure your information. Every time you conduct a bank transaction or simply log into a social media site, all those communications will use cryptography of some description.

An important distinction to make when talking about cryptocurrencies is that cryptocurrencies and blockchain are not the same thing. Blockchain is the technology that enables cryptocurrencies to exist. Often when people say that crypto is a disruptive technology that will change many industries, they have not properly understood the distinction between blockchain and cryptocurrencies. Blockchain as a technology is a very wide subject which has many other uses beyond cryptocurrencies.

Why were cryptocurrencies invented?

Bitcoin was the first cryptocurrency to become mainstream and successful. It came about after the 2008 financial crisis. This was caused in part by massive, risky sub-prime mortgage lending in the US. These extremely risky loans were packaged up, given AAA credit ratings and sold to banks around the world who believed they were buying a much lower risk investment. When interest rates in the US rose, mortgage defaults became rampant. After a few years banks all over the world that owned these loans soon realised that the "safe" mortgage bundles they had purchased were essentially worthless. This caused a drop in the liquidity of banks who then could lend less money to people and business that needed it. Exports plummeted as businesses couldn't access capital, house prices crashed because buyers couldn't access loans and because less people could afford to buy and consumer confidence was damaged leading to less people spending money causing more businesses to fail. During this, many ordinary people lost jobs and homes and it took years for economies to recover.

This financial crisis was blamed on greedy and corrupt bankers who manipulated the monetary system to their advantage in order to claim large bonuses at the expense of regular people. Governments all over the world paid out billions of their tax payers' money to these banks in order to keep them from failing. The very people that were robbed by these banks were then forced to bail them out. To top it all off, very few of the people that played a part in the corruption were punished for doing so. This all helped to create a fundamental mistrust of the modern banking system which was the perfect environment for the first cryptocurrencies to succeed and become mainstream for the first time.

No one knows exactly who invented Bitcoin but it is said their motivation was the perceived injustices of the 2008 recession. They wanted to create a currency that was free from what was seen as the corruption and manipulation of wealthy bankers and politicians. They succeeded and Bitcoin was born. Bitcoin was the first cryptocurrency to be truly decentralised. It is completely free from control of any central authority. A finite number of Bitcoins exist and will ever exist. Bitcoin also had a number of other advantages such as it being impossible to counterfeit or double spend and that its users have complete anonymity when using it. In reality, the causes of the 2008 financial crisis wouldn't have been avoided by using a decentralised currency. The problem wasn't caused by the currency, it was caused by the reckless lending of the currency to people who would never have been able to pay it back.

The lifecycle of a cryptocurrency

At the time of writing there were more than 4000 cryptocurrencies in existence. This begs the question; where do they all come from?

Most cryptocurrencies tend to follow the same lifecycle, centred on an initial coin offering (ICO). An ICO is a mechanism for the creators of the cryptocurrency to monetise their cryptocurrency to fund whatever cryptocurrency development project they claim to be working on.

There are three stages to launching: Pre ICO, ICO and post ICO.

During the pre ICO stage, the creators will aggressively market the ICO to potential investors. They will usually have written a whitepaper detailing how their cryptocurrency is different from the 4000 already out there and that this one will be the one that becomes widely adopted and changes the world. There are a number of tactics used to generate interest in the ICO. Common marketing tactics include a kind of bounty marketing where a person is awarded a cryptocurrency bounty for sharing and promoting the ICO. Another common way of generating interest is by holding an "airdrop" where the creators will offer a small amount of free cryptocurrency tokens to people who want to take part.

During the ICO stage, investors are invited to exchange money for ownership of cryptocurrency tokens. Investors buy the tokens directly from the creators, usually at this stage, it is not possible to trade the tokens as they will not yet be listed on any cryptocurrency exchanges.

After the ICO stage, one of two things usually happens. In the first situation, the cryptocurrency gains enough support and demand to be listed on some cryptocurrency exchanges. This then gives the investors access to the "greater fools" needed to sell their tokens to. If it doesn't get listed on any exchanges, investors can't sell it to anyone and are stuck with nothing. Even if the first situation happens and the cryptocurrency is listed on some exchanges, it doesn't guarantee the cryptocurrency will increase in price. The most common thing to happen is that the price simply drops and the creators run off with all the money they made during the ICO.

Cryptocurrency ICO's are often just pump and dump schemes where they are aggressively marketed by their creators, they create hype to pull in investors, the price rises with the increased demand and then the creators sell all their holdings or "dump" them onto the market and leave investors holding something completely worthless.

Chapter 3:

Busting cryptocurrency myths

Now that we know the basics of what currencies and cryptocurrencies actually are, it's time to address some of the common arguments that crop in in order to justify the sky high prices of cryptocurrencies today. Many cryptocurrency advocates say things like cryptocurrencies are a good investment, they are a good store of value, a good currency or they are more secure than fiat currencies and therefore are not Ponzi schemes.

In this chapter we will debunk those arguments and look at what the reality actually is.

Cryptocurrencies are not investments

One of the most popular arguments for buying cryptocurrencies is that people say they are investments. An investment is an asset acquired with the goal of generating income or appreciation.

When you buy cryptocurrencies, you are not investing, you are speculating. Cryptocurrencies unlike other investments such as stocks or real estate does not generate any cash flow or earnings. They only increase in value due to market inefficiencies and not through underlying value.

Cryptocurrencies do not produce anything in order to create value and increase in price. Stocks for example, represent a share of ownership in a business. When you buy a stock, you are buying an entitlement to a portion of the future earnings of that business. When that business makes a profit, the stock holder is entitled to a portion of those profits, the stock price therefore increases in value. Real estate as another example, generates cash flow through rental income and because the supply of real estate is finite, its price tends to increase year to year as long as demand remains stable.

Fundamentally in order for something to be considered an investment, it should have some sort of standalone value. If you couldn't easily trade the asset, it should still be capable of generating value. A house is still a valuable asset even if you couldn't sell it; you can generate rental income from it or live in it. A stock can still be a valuable asset even if you couldn't sell it; it would generate dividend income.

Cryptocurrencies do not generate any income for their owners therefore cryptocurrency is completely worthless if you couldn't easily sell it. The only thing driving the up the value of cryptocurrencies is the greater fool theory. That is, the idea that every buyer buys the asset in the belief they can sell it to someone else for a higher price who also believes they can sell it on for a higher price and so on.

The continued increase in price relies on a never ending chain of "fools" willing to pay a higher and higher price. This is all well and good but here's the catch; there is a finite number of fools. We already know what happens to Ponzi schemes when they run out of fools. When the buyers dry up, the people left holding the cryptocurrency get the pleasure of watching their investment go down like the Titanic.

Therein lies an incredible risk with cryptocurrencies; at any moment the government of the country you live in could ban, restrict or regulate the trade of any cryptocurrency. If cryptocurrencies get more difficult or impossible to trade, they are worthless as they generate no revenue. This is a very real risk as increased regulation in the cryptocurrency industry is inevitably around the corner. The fact that most of cryptocurrencies actual use is in illicit transactions and the fact that so many retail investors are being scammed by "pump and dump" cryptocurrency start-ups means increased regulation is a foregone conclusion.

With some asset classes like commodities, scarcity is a big driver for the increase in price. Some will point to the scarcity of cryptocurrencies such as Bitcoin and compare it to gold as an asset because of this. The problem with this argument is that cryptocurrencies are not scarce. Bitcoin for example, at the time of writing has had 105 "forks". This means that there are 105 versions of Bitcoin out there in circulation. You could buy another version of Bitcoin that is essentially exactly the same thing for much less than the price of Bitcoin. There is nothing stopping anyone from simply copying Bitcoins source code and making as many exact copies of it as they wanted. You cannot copy productive, revenue generating investments. If it was possible to make copies of any other asset the way you can for cryptocurrencies, they too would be completely worthless.

Cryptocurrencies make terrible currencies

One of the first reasons to buy cryptocurrencies was that they were touted to be the next generation of currencies.

If you've been paying attention, you'll remember that the fundamental purpose of a currency is to facilitate trade. Cryptocurrencies are terrible at this. Regular fiat currencies are in fact very good at facilitating trade. They are widely accepted with stable value, they are secure, portable and well regulated.

Cryptocurrencies have none of these properties. Imagine large shipments of good travelling around the world. If goods were traded using cryptocurrencies as payment rather than the US dollar for example, by the time a ship carrying goods gets to its destination, the value of those goods when measured in cryptocurrencies could be different by orders of magnitude due to the extreme volatility of cryptocurrencies.

To illustrate this, take the example of going to your local supermarket and paying for your shopping using either a fiat currency or a cryptocurrency.

With a fiat currency, you can go to the shop, get to the till, tap your contactless bank card on the card reader and walk out the door.

The same transaction with cryptocurrencies looks very different. Take Bitcoin as an example, it is the most widely accepted cryptocurrency at the time of writing. At the end of 2020, around 2,300 businesses accepted Bitcoin as a form of payment. This sounds like a lot until you learn that there are 32.5 million businesses in the US. The most widely accepted cryptocurrency is accepted in 0.007% of businesses in the US. When you see the numbers in that context, the scale of the problem here is obvious.

In most cases, in order to spend cryptocurrencies, you'll need to value your goods against a fiat currency in order to agree on a price. To do this, you or the shop would need to get a live exchange rate from a cryptocurrency exchange, you would then have to convert the price of your shopping in a fiat currency to a price in your chosen cryptocurrency, apply that conversation to the value of your shopping, then log into your online cryptocurrency wallet, type in the shops wallet address and send the agreed amount.

This transaction will then not be confirmed until the "ledger" of that cryptocurrency is updated. This can take anywhere from minutes to hours. You could not leave the shop with your goods until that transaction was confirmed. The other thing to consider is that in order to complete a transaction, you have to pay a transaction fee. You can of course speed up transactions by paying a higher transaction fee. Either way, you will have to wait for a period of time for the transaction to be confirmed.

Compare the two situations above. Which is situation do you think is the most efficient and easy way of completing the transaction? Some would argue that instead, you would use one of the services that are popping up that can link your cryptocurrency wallet to a contactless card in a similar way to your normal bank card. There are still huge problems that would arise if these kinds of services were widespread. These services are still using fiat currencies to pay for the goods, not cryptocurrencies. When you use your crypto bank card, it just converts cryptocurrencies to fiat currencies and pays using the fiat currency.

If you were to pay solely using cryptocurrencies, the extreme price swings of cryptocurrencies minute to minute would make it extremely hard to agree on prices for goods. You could walk into a shop and the goods could cost double the amount in cryptocurrencies by the time you leave. Imagine being in a world where a loaf of bread needed to have a "live", constantly updated price on it because the currency you were using fluctuated in value so much.

In short even if you manage to solve the huge problems with wide acceptance and general ease of use, cryptocurrencies still don't work as currencies because of their extreme volatility, high transaction cost and slow transaction speeds.

The only way that cryptocurrencies can be involved with every day transactions is by involving fiat currencies and converting between them. This just introduces more steps into the process of a transaction making it less efficient and introducing more middlemen to take a cut of the transaction.

It isn't even a close competition. Fiat currencies are simply better at facilitating trade and always will be. Fiat currencies will always be required in any every day real world transactions. Any use of cryptocurrencies in these transactions in reality, is just adding cost and is just a novelty. In a world where the likes of VISA can send money around the world in a fraction of a second for next to nothing, there is just no need for expensive, slow, volatile cryptocurrencies.

Another important point to consider is that if a country adopted a cryptocurrency with a fixed supply like Bitcoin for example, that countries government would lose the ability to control the supply of money during hard times. Imagine the United States had used Bitcoin as its currency during the 2020 pandemic. The government would not have been able to increase the supply of money and in doing so, pay the massive amounts of stimulus money to keep businesses afloat, people in jobs and in their homes. The lockdown would not have been able to work as people would have been forced to work no matter what or they would lose their homes. A lockdown without financial support from the government would have completely collapsed the economy. As a result of a failed lockdown, the virus would have been able to spread freely and likely kill millions.

Cryptocurrencies do not work as currencies in hypothetical scenarios where they are widely adopted or where they are not widely adopted, they are a novelty.

Cryptocurrencies can be lost forever

The next myth that proliferates around cryptocurrencies is that they are safe and secure, after all, they have the word "crypto" in them so they must be secure , right?

In order to use cryptocurrencies, you need to have a cryptocurrency wallet. Cryptocurrency wallets don't actually store any cryptocurrency, they store information required to interact with a blockchain in order to send or receive cryptocurrencies. This consists of a public key, private key and address on the blockchain. Remember that a blockchain is a list of transactions, it is a record of which wallets control each and every "token" on that blockchain.

Only the public wallet keys associated with each "token" are recorded on the blockchain. In order to control any "token" you need to know the private key associated with the public key. Therein lies the big problem with cryptocurrency wallets; if you lose your private key or someone else manages to steal it, you will never be able to access your cryptocurrency again.

In June 2021, the FBI announced that they were able to steal back a ransom that a US company, Colonial Pipelines had paid to cyber attackers after their systems were compromised with a ransomware attack. Colonial Pipelines had paid $4.4 million to a group of hackers on the 8th May 2021. Less than a month later, the FBI's Digital Extortion Taskforce was able to take back $2.3 million of the ransom that was paid to the hackers Bitcoin wallets. It is unknown how the FBI managed to do this but it just highlights the fact that cryptocurrency wallets are not at all secure. If the FBI can do this to a group of experienced hackers who no doubt are very well versed in good cyber security practises, then no wallet is really safe.

There are three types of cryptocurrency wallet, each solves one of these issues whilst leaving it vulnerable to the other issue. Software wallets, are stored on your PC or online. They are usually protected by a password you can choose. If you forget your password for an online wallet, you can usually recover your password and therefore access to your cryptocurrency. The downside of this however, is that software wallets are vulnerable to viruses and hackers. If a hacker cracks your password or a virus deletes your hard drive for example, you'll lose everything.

Another type of wallet, a hardware wallet can be used. This involves storing your wallet on a hard drive or similar device that is completely disconnected from the internet, putting your cryptocurrency beyond the reach of viruses and hackers. The downside is, it also puts it beyond your reach until you connect it to the internet again. The other downside is that the failure or loss of the physical storage device will result in you losing everything.

The third type of wallet is called a paper wallet. These involve printing your keys on a physical piece of paper. These put your cryptocurrencies beyond the reach of hackers and virus and also get around the issue of the physical failure of a storage device. It is however, still easy to lose or damage that piece of paper. Paper is also not renowned for its hard wearing properties. Again, if you damage or lose that piece of paper, you'll lose everything.

There are countless stories of people losing access to funds stored in cryptocurrency wallets that were either lost, stolen or damaged in some way.

Imagine the hard drive you stored your life savings Bitcoin wallet was destroyed in a fire or was stolen or your two year old threw it in the bin without you noticing? Or imagine you were completely human and forgot your password? You could lose everything and not have any means of recovering your cryptocurrency. With fiat currencies, if you keep your money in a bank, it is safe. If someone steals your bank card details and uses it, your bank will refund you. If you forget your pin or password, your bank can confirm your identity and give you access to your money again. If your wallet goes in the bin, you can order new bank cards (assuming you don't carry your life savings around in your wallet).

There have been countless events where investors have lost everything due to loss, theft or fraud.

One famous theft example was the compromise of the cryptocurrency exchange, Mt. Gox. In February 2014, hackers managed to steal 840,000 Bitcoin from the exchange and its customers. This was valued at a staggering $460 million at the time. This brought about the possibility of increased regulation and dented investors' confidence in cryptocurrencies. It took years for the industry to recover from the reputational damage from this event. The threat of events like this happening again is still there and it presents a major risk when dealing with cryptocurrencies.

Another notable major loss of cryptocurrency occurred in 2018 with the death of Gerald Cotton, the founder of Canada's largest cryptocurrency exchange. Gerald was allegedly the only person who knew the cryptographic keys needed to unlock the exchanges cold wallets. As a result, $190 million worth of users' cryptocurrency was lost forever. This same founder allegedly had run his own Ponzi scheme prior to starting the cryptocurrency exchange. There is speculation to this day that he is in fact alive and enjoying the $190 million that was supposedly lost forever.

As recently as April 2021, the boss of a cryptocurrency exchange based in Turkey disappeared promoting fears that he had eloped with investors funds. This is estimated to be about $2 billion worth of cryptocurrencies. In March 2021, the exchange had ran a promotion where they offered new signups millions of free Dogecoins, a popular, meme inspired cryptocurrency. Most have reported to have never received these. One could speculate that this offer was simply to draw users in to deposit their cryptocurrencies before the boss disappeared with billions of their dollars.

It seems that nowhere is really safe in the cryptocurrency world, there is always a very real risk of losing everything. The cryptocurrency world due to its anonymous nature is full of fraud. Compromises such as the ones above are an unsurprisingly common occurrence. These kinds of events expose the real weakness of the decentralisation argument for cryptocurrencies. The lax security and lack of regulation of these centralised services exposes investors to enormous risk. Banks give their users a level of safety guaranteed. If you lose access to your bank account, you can always recover access to it. If someone steals from your bank account, the bank will refund you as long as it wasn't due to your carelessness. No such guarantees exist in the world of cryptocurrencies.

The very fact that cryptocurrencies are often held and traded in centralised exchanges and wallets makes the decentralisation argument for cryptocurrencies void anyway. In essence, by using cryptocurrencies instead of fiat currencies, you are simply trading the security, accessibility and stability of your fiat currency for the volatility, risk and hassle of using cryptocurrencies. You are likely going to pay deposit and transaction fees along the way too.

Cryptocurrency exchanges

Cryptocurrency advocates will tell you that cryptocurrency exchanges are much better than they used to be and that nowadays they are much safer to use. If you want to use cryptocurrencies, you will have to use an exchange at some point but there are a lot of potential problems with these exchanges.

You need a cryptocurrency exchange in order to practically trade and use cryptocurrencies. A cryptocurrency exchange is a place where you can exchange fiat currencies for cryptocurrencies and cryptocurrencies for other cryptocurrencies. There are a lot of problems with these exchanges, some of which we have already discussed, namely cyber security, fraud, liquidity and regulation.

It seems ironic that in order to trade your decentralised cryptocurrency, you must use a centralised, unregulated exchange that could be operated anonymously by anyone with no auditable or enforceable cyber security practices. Using a mainstream bank is simply easier, much less risky and much more efficient.

To make matters worse, on top of the risks already discussed, these exchanges have shown themselves to be extremely unreliable when the markets are turbulent. During the cryptocurrency market crash during May 2021, a lot of exchanges halted trading due to the high volume of transactions. Where have we seen similar patterns of investors being prevented from withdrawing funds when many investors are withdrawing funds?

It wouldn't surprise me if some cryptocurrency exchanges were in themselves Ponzi schemes where the owners of the exchange are paying themselves handsomely with investors' money that is deposited. The problem is that, there is no way of knowing until the market has a prolonged crash and these exchanges start failing. It just adds another dimension of risk to an already risky investment practise.

The language the leaders of these exchanges have used during the May 2021 crash is also concerning. They release statements apologising for their customers not being able to trade and then attribute it to people "buying the dip". One cryptocurrency exchange CEO released a statement saying that cryptocurrencies were "selling at 30-50% sale, resulting in high user traffic".

This kind of language is clearly intended to create a fear of missing out and encourage investors to buy assets that are tumbling in price. If the cryptocurrencies these people were pedalling were really that good, they would not have to make statements like that to rope people in. Can you imagine the same statements coming from a regulated bank or financial institution? Of course not, it is incredibly misleading and potentially damaging to investors.

Business practises like this just highlight the risks investors take in trusting people like this with their money. No cryptocurrency exchange is going to be honest acknowledging any negatives about cryptocurrencies because that is where they make their money. They want you to keep buying and trading no matter what. Encouraging investors to act the way they did just speaks to their untrustworthiness.

If a guy in the street offered you an investment opportunity that was 30-50% off, you wouldn't just hand him all your money would you? Why then when some guy that operates a cryptocurrency exchange that could disappear without a trace at any time offers an investment opportunity at 30-50% off, people are fine with it?

Environmental impact

One myth that is starting to creep up is that cryptocurrencies can be mined sustainably. The environmental impact of cryptocurrencies is huge. The mining of cryptocurrencies is very energy intensive. In March 2021, it was estimated that the energy consumption of Bitcoin alone is around 125 terawatt hours annually. All the worlds' data centres are estimated to use about 205 terawatt hours annually. This means that Bitcoin alone uses almost as much energy as the rest of the internet worldwide.

To put this another way, this is about the same energy consumption as a country the size of Norway. To make matters worse, Bitcoin only accounts for about half of the global cryptocurrency market. So really, cryptocurrencies most likely use more energy annually than the rest of the internet. That is a shocking statistic and it is only set to grow.

Bitcoin mining by design is fundamentally energy intensive. When computers mine Bitcoin, what they're fundamentally doing is updating the ledger of Bitcoin transactions or the "blockchain". This requires them to solve extremely difficult numerical puzzles. For each new block on the blockchain, the first machine to find the solution is rewarded with a set number of Bitcoin. The whole process then starts again for the next block. The Bitcoin network is designed so that on average, a new block is mined every 10 minutes. Bitcoin mining computers around the world are constantly competing to be the first to solve the next block and earn Bitcoin in return.

To take advantage of the high Bitcoin price, new mining computers are being added to the network every day in an effort to make money. As the mining potential of the Bitcoin network increases, so does the difficulty of solving the numerical puzzles needed to earn Bitcoin. This means that the energy required to mine each Bitcoin is always increasing. To compound this problem, every 210,000 blocks (about every 4 years) the number of Bitcoins awarded per block is halved. To earn the same number of Bitcoins as before, Bitcoin miners will need to have double the processing power and so more mining computers will be added to the network, further increasing the mining difficulty and energy consumption.

In Bitcoins case, if it were to be adopted as a global reserve currency, the price of Bitcoin would be so high that the world's electricity production would have to double to power the miners required to process the transactions. Clearly that is not going to happen. Electricity generation capacity is the fundamental limit that makes mass adoption of Bitcoin essentially impossible.

The dependence on huge amounts of cheap electricity drives the environmental disaster. If energy prices rise, it becomes more expensive to mine Bitcoin. At some point, the cost of mining will be higher than the reward in Bitcoin.

This tends to mean that Bitcoin mining usually takes place in areas where electricity is cheap. Today, a majority of Bitcoin mining takes place in China where cheap electricity is produced using coal fired power stations. Electricity generation using coal is the most environmentally damaging method, it accounts for more pollution than any other energy source.

The sad irony of this issue is that a large proportion of cryptocurrency advocates are millennials who care about green issues and might not actually be aware of the huge environmental impact that cryptocurrencies have. Bitcoin just doesn't scale, it is inefficient by design and in a world where our existence is threatened by climate change, it will never become widely adopted and accepted. It is a bubble that will burst eventually. All bubbles burst eventually and it could just be the environmental concerns around cryptocurrencies that do it.

Regulation risks

Some cryptocurrency advocates argue either that increased regulation will not happen or that it will actually help the industry. The lack of regulation in the cryptocurrency industry has created an environment where Ponzi schemes can flourish. This doesn't mean that this will continue forever. Inevitably, when enough people get ripped off, national financial regulators will eventually have to act to protect investors. The proliferation of Ponzi schemes, fraud and massive cybersecurity problems will not go unchecked forever. This is one of the biggest threats to cryptocurrencies today.

It is currently unknown what any potential regulation would look like, how it would be enforced and who would enforce it. If regulators started cracking down in a meaningful way on cryptocurrency exchanges or regulated cryptocurrency start-ups, it is not known what will happen to the market.

For example, if more stringent anti money laundering regulations were applied to cryptocurrencies, this would essentially remove the biggest real world use case for cryptocurrencies. If you remove the biggest use case for cryptocurrencies, this is likely to negatively impact the price.

Another possibility is that the use of cryptocurrencies could be banned or restricted in some way. For example, restricting institutions from trading in cryptocurrencies has just been announced by Chinas central bank. Any restrictions on the trade and use of cryptocurrencies will reduce the potential investment pool and make wide adoption harder and less likely.

There is also the possibility that increased regulation when it comes will improve the market and make it safer for investors, encouraging more to join in. Realistically though, if a well-regulated cryptocurrency is going to hit the market, it isn't going to be the cryptocurrency ICO that you saw advertised on Twitter last week. It is going to be a cryptocurrency that is introduced by a central bank.

We can only guess at what regulation will come into force and what affect that will have on the market. No one really knows for sure. This is a big risk and one that should not be taken lightly when considering an investment. If there was a threat that electric cars would be banned, would you still invest in Tesla? Of course not, you'd be completely mad. Why then would you consider an investment in cryptocurrency if that same threat exists?

It is possible that blockchain technology will have a role to play in the future world currency market, but it will still be fiat currency based, backed and implemented by central banks. At a fundamental level, no stable government in the world is going to accept taxes paid in a cryptocurrency that they don't regulate and control themselves. The only way a government would implement the use of a currency they don't control would be in a hyperinflation situation which tends to happen during periods of intense political instability. This means that if cryptocurrencies became widely adopted in your country, you would have much bigger problems to deal with as your counties economy in this situation is most likely very weak.

An example would be the announcement in 2021 that El Salvador would be the first country in the world to classify Bitcoin as legal tender. On the face of it, people would say that this was a good endorsement for Bitcoin. When you consider the fact that as of 2017, 29% of people in El Salvador lived in poverty and that the GDP per capita in El Salvador was $4,187 in 2019 (the US for comparison was $65,287 in the same year), it does not exactly paint the picture of a big win for Bitcoin.

When weighing up the probability of regulation helping or hindering the unregulated cryptocurrency market that exists today, it is likely that the regulation will hinder the cryptocurrency market. Thinking about it logically, governments and central banks are not going to give away control of their monetary systems and everything that goes with it. The ability of central banks to control the supply of money through changing interest rates and quantitative easing is incredibly important to the stable functioning of economies all over the world. In a world where governments could not influence their monetary policies, recessions when they happen would be much deeper, longer and cause much more poverty. Central banks and governments will act to protect their monetary systems to protect their own citizens in future. The current cryptocurrency market will be looked back on in years to come as a "crypto protest" caused by the 2008 financial crisis. Governments will improve their economic management and slowly regain trust. Couple that with cryptocurrency regulation intended to protect monetary systems and the cryptocurrency bubble could burst.

Cryptocurrencies are not a store of value

With Bitcoins value soaring and the obvious issues with its utility as a currency becoming more widely known. Enthusiasts are now saying that cryptocurrencies are a store of value and not a currency. The problem with this is that cryptocurrencies don't work as a store of value. For something to be a good store of value, it has to be liquid, universally accepted and have a stable price.

Cryptocurrencies have none of these characteristics. We have already discussed the issues around the universal acceptance of cryptocurrencies and as we've seen, it's a huge challenge that looks incredibly unlikely to be overcome. In terms of price stability, it is not uncommon to see prices to fluctuate by 100's of percent day to day for some cryptocurrencies. Again, using Bitcoin as an example, the top 100 Bitcoin wallets are believed to hold 13% of the total Bitcoin supply. This leaves the risk of the market being flooded at any time and causing massive volatility at any time.

The last challenge around cryptocurrencies as a store of value is their liquidity. This aspect is more difficult to evaluate as it can change from day to day. In general though, if you've ever tried to convert a cryptocurrency to fiat currency, you'll actually find it quite difficult to get the cash into your bank account. Some cryptocurrencies can suffer from low liquidity which makes it hard to trade them. If there are no buyers in the market, you have no one to sell to and are therefore stuck with your cryptocurrency. Even assuming the market for the cryptocurrency in question is liquid at the time, you still have transaction fees to pay and then you have to physically withdraw the fiat currency to your bank account.

This now involves anti money laundering checks which can take quite a long time depending on the cryptocurrency exchange you choose to use. Withdrawals are also usually subject to minimum amounts, restricted to certain currencies and again often have fees associated with them. Cryptocurrencies are not as liquid as you first think, it is easy to get money into them but not necessarily easy to get it out. Try a small amount yourself as an example and follow the process of depositing fiat currency, exchanging for cryptocurrency, exchanging back to fiat currency and withdrawing. You will see it is both costly and time consuming and clearly does not represent a liquid asset.

Cryptocurrencies are not commodities

Some investors like to compare cryptocurrencies with commodities like gold when justifying their investment. There are a lot of problems with this. They both have completely different properties. Gold has unique properties and is considered a hybrid commodity in that it is both a currency and a commodity. It deserves a mention of its own as it is one of the oldest types of investment. Humans have attributed value to gold for thousands of years because of its scarcity and physical properties. The scarcity of gold is important as this means there is almost a fixed amount of it in the market. There is very little risk of a supplier suddenly flooding the market with gold as is possible with cryptocurrencies. The scarcity of gold is a physical limit that no one can change whereas cryptocurrencies as we've seen, are not scarce at all.

Gold is an unreactive metal and as such it does not tarnish and is therefore attractive in appearance. This is why it has been used to produce items of value such as coins and jewellery for thousands of years. It is estimated that about 38% of golds demand is due to the jewellery industry. It also has limited uses in electronics and medicine. In other words, gold has practical uses that justify its value. If the demand for gold as a store of value disappeared overnight, there would still be demand for it for other applications. The same cannot be said of cryptocurrencies. They are not a physical item and they have no physical real world use that could make them valuable as anything other than a currency.

Until this century, most currencies were backed up by physical gold. Although most currencies are no longer backed by the "gold standard" any more, most people still believe gold has value. As a result, gold is seen as a good way to mitigate or "hedge" against inflation. Whilst the supply of currencies and goods tends to go up and therefore inflation with it, the supply of gold is very limited and so it holds its value. Over a long period of time, gold is seen as a relatively low risk investment. Gold is considered lower risk because its relatively fixed supply means the value of gold tends to rise.

Gold has been engrained in human culture over thousands of years, it has some limited uses as a material, a limited supply and is generally stable in price. There are therefore not many similarities between cryptocurrencies and gold.

Why decentralised finance doesn't work

One of the biggest arguments I see in favour of cryptocurrencies is the decentralisation argument. Decentralised finance is the concept of replacing traditional financial institutions such as brokerages, exchanges and banks with a blockchain solution that allows users to deal directly with each other. The idea behind this is that you cut out the middle man and therefore earn higher interest rates as an investor and pay lower rates as a borrower. The other driver behind cutting out banks is the deep distrust of the banking system a lot of people still have after the 2008 financial crisis.

The biggest problem with decentralised finance as a concept is that at its most basic level, it cannot work unless the currency behind it is adopted and backed by a central bank or government. As we've already seen, unless the currency is adopted everywhere, right up to being able to pay your taxes using it, it is useless. The other major issue is the ability of lenders to access collateral on loans. With a decentralised, cryptocurrency based system, you borrow cryptocurrency and put up cryptocurrency as collateral. That's like going to the bank and asking for a mortgage for $100,000 but giving them $120,000 as collateral. The whole point of the loan is to allow you to borrow against an asset you are purchasing. If the lender cannot have a claim to that collateral, the whole contract is useless.

The concept of being able to borrow or lend money and getting more favourable interest rates by cutting out middlemen sound great, but you have to consider what that really means in practise. Often ideas that sound great in principle, do not actually work in real world applications.

Take the example of a mortgage to buy a house. Traditionally, the customer will go to the bank and apply for the loan, the bank will check their credit history and the affordability of the loan they are asking for. They also check the value of the property that is being purchased to ensure that if the customer defaults on the loan, the property can be sold in order to recover the money. As part of the legal transfer of the property, the bank will have a claim to the property in the event that the loan is not repaid in line with the loan agreement. All these checks are regulated by governments and financial authorities and have developed over a hundred years to give the right balance or risk to both the banks and their customers. These financial regulations exist to protect both parties in the transaction and are fundamental to the smooth running of our modern economies.

Now consider the same case in a decentralised financial system. The first issue in this case is the adoption of the cryptocurrency. If it is not backed by the government or central bank, who in their right mind is going to accept it as payment for something as valuable as a house? The answer is no one and so let's assume that we are going to pay using a fiat currency.

When the customer goes to get the loan for the property, they have to put up more than the loans value in cryptocurrency as collateral. The decentralised lending facilities available at the time of writing required collateral worth double the fiat currency loan amount. Let's ignore the obvious problem with that and assume the customer has the collateral and they get the loan, paid as fiat currency. Once the customer gets the money, they transfer it to the property owner who then transfers ownership of the property to the customer.

In the case of a decentralised financial system based on cryptocurrencies, the collateral on the loan will not be the property but will instead be an amount of cryptocurrency. The ability of the lender to have a claim on any physical assets in the event of the customer not paying back the loan is out of the question in a decentralised system. So what happens then when the loan does not get paid back? The lender gets the collateral that was put up for the loan.

The problem here is obvious; it's a terrible deal for the customer. The first big issue is that they need to hold double the loans value in collateral in order to get the loan. Imagine a first time home buyer wanting to buy a house for £100,000. In a decentralised system, they would need £200,000 in cryptocurrency assets in order to get the loan. This completely defeats the purpose of the loan and in a real economy, will be useless to a vast majority of people. With a bank loan, all they need is a 5% deposit or £5,000 as the bank uses the property as collateral. Mortgage lending is a foundation of modern economies and relies on the lender having access to the properties as collateral.

Another big problem is that the interest rates are actually terrible too despite what the cryptocurrency advocates would have you believe. At the time of writing, a popular decentralised cryptocurrency lender offered loans starting at 4.5% APR. In comparison, at the same time, banks are offering loans starting at 1.44% APR.

The irony of a cryptocurrency based decentralised financial system is that it still relies on a fiat currency in order to operate and so it is not truly decentralised. There is no getting away from the fact that centralised banking systems are not the terrible, evil thing many would have you believe. A centralised banking system is what allows you to buy your home or car. It allows you to get paid a currency that is stable in value and therefore allows you to buy the things you need to live; food, shelter, energy and security. Centralised financial systems put man on the moon, they allow your job to exist, they allow roads to get built, they allow hospitals, schools, emergency services and government all to exist. Modern centralised financial systems are what allow our society to exist as it does today.

When you add the risk, terrible interest rates, ridiculous collateral requirements, volatility and lack of regulation that a decentralised financial system would have, it is hard to see how anyone in a developed country in reality would seriously adopt it. Despite what you have been led to believe, our financial systems actually serve us very well as they are and although events like the 2008 financial crisis are a product of this type of system, regulations adapt to make these events less likely and less damaging.

Cryptocurrencies often fail

Cryptocurrency start-ups are often called great investment opportunities. Investors are encouraged to blindly buy in to the next Bitcoin early and then they will be rich next week. The reality couldn't be more different. According to the website deadcoins.com, as of May 2021, there over 1,600 failed cryptocurrencies. These failed cryptocurrencies are sorted into groups under the headings "deceased", "hacks", "scams" or "parodies". In this case, the term failed means that they have extremely low trading volumes or have experienced a severe drop in price that they have not recovered from. When you consider that as of May 2021, there are about 4,000 cryptocurrencies in existence, it paints a bleak picture for the future of cryptocurrencies. 40% of all cryptocurrencies that have existed so far have failed.

Many cryptocurrencies start and end the same way. Some land on the scene to great fanfare and eventually fade to nothing once investors realise there is no working or unique product. Some fail when lax security allows hackers to steal millions. Others fail simply because they fail to generate a following online. The point is that the success of a cryptocurrency isn't due to any sort of fundamental value, it's down to its perception in the wider market.

Investing in a cryptocurrency start up is like playing roulette at a casino. You are relying on the cryptocurrency to be marketed effectively online to other people who think they will also make money out of it. If the cryptocurrency fails to generate hype and momentum, it will soon join the other 1,600 failed cryptocurrencies.

Chapter 4:

Crypto, the greatest Ponzi scheme

Similarities between crypto and Ponzi schemes

When looking at Ponzi schemes and cryptocurrencies, you don't have to look very hard to spot similarities between them. As a reminder, a Ponzi scheme is a form of investment fraud that lures investors in and pays early investors with funds from more recent investors. Ponzi schemes generate no legitimate earnings and therefore require a constant stream of new investors to survive. There is really no difference between that and a vast majority of cryptocurrencies. Cryptocurrencies do not generate any revenue and there is no asset behind them that is of any use and so the only way for an investor to get a return from cryptocurrencies is simply to sell them to another investor for a higher price. The Securities and Exchange Commission (SEC) in the USA published a list of warning signs to look out for when considering whether an investment is a Ponzi scheme, cryptocurrencies flag up on several of those points.

Ponzi scheme red flags

The SEC defines several characteristics of Ponzi schemes to watch out for. They say that when considering an investment, investors should consider whether their investment passes these checks or not. If not, the investment should be avoided or advice from a reputable, independent and qualified financial professional. These characteristics are:

1. The promise of high returns with little or no risk. Every investment carries risk and generally, investments paying higher returns tend to carry higher risk. If an investment is pitched as low risk and high return, you should be suspicious of it. Pretty much every cryptocurrency investment opportunity you will see gives the promise of fast, high returns and little to no mention of the extraordinary risk involved.

2. Overly consistent returns. The returns on pretty much every investment will fluctuate from time to time. An investment that guarantees a positive return regardless of market conditions is something to be wary of. Cryptocurrencies are incredibly volatile in price and so any that promise consistent returns should be a concern.

3. Unregistered investments. Ponzi schemes are typically not registered with regulatory bodies such as the SEC. Lack of registration is a red flag as it shows there is no independent governance or oversight of the investment opportunity. The most likely reason for this is because the investment is illegitimate. There are countless

unregistered and unregulated methods of purchasing cryptocurrencies. This is a major concern and leaves investors extremely vulnerable to Ponzi schemes.

4. Unlicensed sellers. Most regulatory bodies require firms and people selling and dealing with investments to be registered. An unregistered seller or firm implies that there is something illicit that they do not want the authorities to know about. Most individuals that promote cryptocurrency investments online are unregistered and unlicensed. Again, this leaves investors open to falling for the promises and lies of charismatic and popular snake oil salesmen.

5. Secretive, complex strategies. A lot of Ponzi schemes hide behind promises of generating returns through some sort of complex technology or strategy that is hard for ordinary investors to understand. This is a deliberate tactic. Investors should avoid any investment that they do not fully understand. This warning flag is probably the most common one across cryptocurrencies. Most investors do not have a deep understanding of what they are buying, leaving them vulnerable to cryptocurrency Ponzi schemes. A vast majority of investors would have no way of verifying any technical claims a cryptocurrency start-up was making. This means the new, disruptive technology they are investing in might not even exist.

6. Issues with paperwork. Account statement errors or delays are often a sign that funds are not being

invested as promised. Creative accounting and accounting delays are a common feature of cryptocurrencies start-ups until they disappear; another red flag.

7. Difficulty receiving payment. Ponzi schemes often make it difficult for investors to cash out in order to keep the scheme running. Often higher returns are offered to investors to stay in the scheme longer or they simply make it difficult to withdraw money with the guise of lengthy paper work processes or checks. This is a feature of some popular cryptocurrency exchanges. It can take a long time to withdraw money from cryptocurrency exchanges once you have put it in.

Most cryptocurrencies flag up on so many of the points on the SEC's Ponzi scheme list that it is very hard to see how they can be anything other than a Ponzi scheme. Even the most well-known cryptocurrency, Bitcoin, is undoubtedly a Ponzi scheme. The only difference is between Bitcoin and Charles Ponzi's original scheme is that in Bitcoins case, there is no single person in charge. Cryptocurrencies are just decentralised Ponzi schemes.

Pump and dump schemes

Whilst Bitcoin as a Ponzi scheme is relatively long lived (at the time of writing, Bitcoin is still going), a vast majority of cryptocurrencies are short lived "pump and dump" Ponzi schemes. How this works is that a cryptocurrency is set up by a person or people. Usually, this will be a copy, paste and rebrand of an already existing cryptocurrency to keep the process quick, easy and cheap. The developers of this new currency own all of this new currency at the start, meaning if they are able to sell it to anyone, they can make easy money with little to no effort.

Once the cryptocurrency is created, it is then heavily promoted and marketed, often through free to use channels such as social media. The developers create demand by spreading misinformation, false promises of what the technology will achieve and lure investors in with the promise of getting rich quick. Often, these cryptocurrency start-ups can be very successful in building cult followings online. Catch phrases such as "to the moon!" proliferate and build hype and the fear of missing out in people.

Once they have a following, the developers have a pool of people they can make easy money from. The developers will launch a platform or website allowing them to take payments from investors and give them their worthless cryptocurrency in return. Once a platform to sell the cryptocurrency is created, developers can then launch their new cryptocurrency. Investors pile in quickly, raising the price of the cryptocurrency. This phase is called the "pump", as the creators "pump" or "inflate" the price of the cryptocurrency.

This pump phase continues as for as long as the hype from investors lasts. During this time, the developers will be careful not to sell too much on the market in order to keep the price rising. Eventually however, as with all Ponzi schemes, they run out of people to sell it to. When this happens, the "dump" phase is about to begin.

During the "dump" phase, the market is flooded with the cryptocurrency as the creators "dump" their remaining assets onto the market. Some investors, seeing the price drop, will also sell, making the drop more severe. A lot of investors however, are usually so infatuated with their investment that they will refuse to sell and believe that if they continue to hold, the drop will reverse and the price will rise again. This is a tactic employed by people like the developers or people who are flooding the market who actively promote a culture where people will hold onto their investment at all costs, spawning catch phrases like "diamond hands" online to encourage people to hold.

This tactic has the effect of allowing the developers to dump more cryptocurrency on the market and also means that investors are all the more damaged as they hold until the cryptocurrency is completely worthless.

In this example, the pump and dump scheme was operated by the original developers but existing cryptocurrencies can also be manipulated in the same way. A group of scammers might target an unpopular cryptocurrency with very little volume. They buy as much of the cryptocurrency as they can, usually a significant proportion of what is in circulation. They then pump and dump it in the same way as the previous example.

In 2021 in the wake of the GameStop saga which saw the US company GameStop's stock soar 1500% in a matter of days, a new wave of cryptocurrency pump and dump scheme has come about. The fear of missing out has spawned a new generation of pump and dump scheme where an investors goal is actually to pump and dump the cryptocurrency. These new schemes work in a similar way to the previous two examples except that nowadays, they are openly promoted as pump and dump schemes. An investor or group of investors picks a cryptocurrency and buys as much as possible whilst promoting on online forums and messaging apps, encouraging people to get involved in the latest pump and dump scheme. These new schemes end in the same way as the previous examples, with the cryptocurrency being dumped and the price falling through the floor.

So how big a problem is this? A study published in August 2020, identified an estimated 355 examples of suspicious trading activity across several cryptocurrency exchanges over a period of just seven months. For comparison, they found that over a ten year period, you would only expect a couple of hundred examples of similar manipulation in penny stocks. In essence, this means the least regulated and most risky stock investments are more than ten times less likely to be subject to manipulation than a cryptocurrency investment.

OneCoin Ponzi scheme

One of the most notorious cryptocurrency Ponzi schemes managed to rob an estimated $4 billion USD over a period of three years between 2014 and 2017. This cryptocurrency was called OneCoin. The OneCoin scheme was run by a woman called Ruja Ignatova who travelled the world promoting OneCoin to millions of investors. She would organise events that rivalled Apple product launches in world class venues such as Wembley Arena. Ignatova told cheering fans that OneCoin was the Bitcoin killer and that it would become the world's biggest cryptocurrency.

Bitcoin in its life had gone from trading for a few cents per Bitcoin to thousands of dollars per Bitcoin a few years later. This is what Ignatova promised investors in Onecoin, unbelievable returns for no work at all. Ignatova was charismatic and able to convince thousands to hand over their hard earned cash. There are countless examples of people also then convincing their friends and family to join the scheme too.

OneCoin was able to operate at the time as it sold educational materials such as courses on cryptocurrencies and investing. This was considered its main business although it turns out that most of this educational material was plagiarised. This educational business worked as a multilevel marketing scheme where buyers were offered rewards for bringing in more buyers.

There were educational packages available to buy costing from a few hundred dollars, right the way up to hundreds of thousands of dollars. Buyers of these packages were to receive tokens that could be exchanged for OneCoins through an internal OneCoin exchange. Buyers had to buy more than just the bottom level package in order to get access to this exchange. There was still no way of converting OneCoin back to fiat currency once an investor had bought it, but this was constantly delayed and hadn't launched yet.

One of the reasons OneCoin ended up being so popular was that it combined features of a Ponzi scheme and features of a multilevel marketing pyramid scheme. Ignatova recruited seasoned multilevel marketing companies who redirected all the sales people working for them to drop everything and start selling OneCoin instead. This combination turned out to be extremely effective in parting people with their money.

All over the world, investors were investing their savings into OneCoin, hoping to get into the next part of the cryptocurrency revolution. But there was one problem these investors didn't know about. There was no cryptocurrency and no blockchain. The company was taking investors' money without having anything to give back in return. Rumours that OneCoin was a fraud started circulating in 2016 and in the same year, financial institutions started warning that OneCoin was a Ponzi scheme. In the UK for example, the FCA issued a warning on its website about OneCoin and that consumers should be wary of dealing with it. After a year, the warning was removed after the FCA said it had been up long enough. OneCoin advocates jumped on this as confirmation that OneCoin was not a scam. Several events were then held in the UK, scooping up millions more of investors' money in the process.

Ignatova continued touring the world promoting OneCoin for another year roping in many more investors who did not heed the growing warnings and rumours that it was all a scam. Whilst investment in Europe was slowing down, in places like Africa, it was still growing. This scam was truly worldwide and took in people from all social classes in many different countries. From poor farmers in Uganda to wealthy businessmen in the west.

That was until in October 2017, she failed to turn up at an event and instead, simply disappeared along with millions of investors' money.

Inevitably, OneCoin as a company was structured in a way to make it almost impossible to follow where these funds went. Countless anonymous shell companies had been set up to funnel funds all around the world in such a way that it was impossible to track and in essence, the funds had disappeared leaving investors devastated. The international nature of the company and its accounts has made it extremely difficult for authorities in different countries to actually pursue the ones responsible for the scam.

Investors looking back have said that at the time, they had seen or heard about people striking it rich with Bitcoin and had thought OneCoin would be another chance of similar success. Most investors did not understand the technology they were apparently buying into but they saw how Ignatova was presenting at large conference to thousands of people and thought that many people couldn't be wrong. Ignatova had genuine degrees from renowned Universities such as Oxford University and that also helped increase investors trust in her.

It turns out that Ignatova has actually been convicted of fraud in the past. This is something that anyone could have found out with a simple Google search. Investors were all too keen to look at a couple of fancy certificates and believe that no one who graduated from Oxford could be dishonest. Again, this highlights just how little investors actually understood about what they were getting into.

Another method used to keep people investing more and more into the scheme was to prepare them for conversations with sceptics. They were able to sign up to WhatsApp groups where OneCoin employees would give them responses to any arguments against OneCoin. They were told that "Bitcoiners" were "haters" and that they should not believe the outside world as they were merely haters. This had the effect of conditioning investors to believe that their investment was sound and that anyone who said otherwise was doing so because they didn't want them to succeed.

The culture within these groups of investors made it very hard for investors to admit they were wrong, even when presented with evidence that the whole thing was a scam. People not only invested their money but also their belief, reputation and intelligence which made it very hard for people to see the truth in what was going on. The sense of belonging and the belief that they were part of something big created a cult like culture that proved to be extremely damaging.

To date, Ignatova has still not been found and no one really knows where she is. Rumours have her on a yacht in the

Mediterranean and others have her travelling between Moscow and Dubai, protected by powerful friends. Some people connected with OneCoin however, have been jailed including Ignatova's brother, Konstantin Ignatov who was sentenced to 90 years in prison in the US.

Crypto bank Ponzi schemes

Another fairly easy Ponzi scheme to spot in the world of cryptocurrencies is the rise of cryptocurrency based online "banks" that are often touted as the future of a decentralised financial system. In one example, I did not have to look past the home page of their website before alarm bells started ringing. I will not name the company here but for simplicity, I will refer to the company here as "BrickFi".

In this example, on their homepage, they advertise a stellar 8.6% interest rate on cryptocurrency deposited with them. Bear in mind, most savings accounts with mainstream banks are paying about 1% interest on savings accounts at the time of writing. It amazing how familiar this sounds and yet here we are again, in black and white on their fancy website. Despite the first warning flag of returns that exceed any other savings account by many times, I scrolled on down their homepage to see if I had got the wrong impression.

Further down the homepage, I then saw that as well as opening a savings account paying 8.6% interest, you could also take out a loan starting at 4.5% interest. It doesn't take a genius to work out that those numbers don't add up. Look at any other bank in the world and try to find one that can pay more in interest on their savings accounts that they earn from the loans that they give out. I'll make it easy for you; you won't find one.

This is because, at the most basic level, a bank works by paying interest on savings investors have deposited with the bank. In 2021, a saver would do well to get 1% interest on savings with a mainstream bank for example. Now where does the bank get the money to pay these investors their interest? Well, they lend the money that was originally deposited out to other people who pay the bank interest on the loan. In 2021, a borrower could get a personal loan from a bank and expect a good rate of interest to be 2.9%. So the bank gains 2.9% and pays out 1% which means they make 1.9% profit. That is a very simplified explanation of how traditional banks work.

Now, take this exciting new cryptocurrency bank promising 8.6% interest on deposits but only charging 4.5% interest on loans. That means they're losing on average 4.1%. Again, it doesn't take Warren Buffet to tell you that this company's balance sheet will not add up.

This company raises so many of the red flags of the SEC's Ponzi scheme red flags to watch out for. Straight off the bat, they promise stellar returns for a low risk savings account. This is the first red flag. The second red flag is that those returns are promised to be a consistent 8.6%.

The third issue actually is a combination of three warning flags on the SEC's list. These are problems with their paperwork, the fact that they are unregistered sellers and that their investments are unregistered. They are in fact unregistered as an investment company despite it looking that way at first glance. Whilst they are registered with the SEC as a "pooled investment fund", a simple Google search and 30 second look at their SEC filing shows that they are not actually registered as an investment company under the Investment Company Act of 1940. This means they are exempt from a lot of regulatory oversight. It is only when reading deep into the small print on their website that they disclose the fact that their savings account is not subject to the financial protections of any regulatory body and that total loss of principal is possible.

The fourth red flag is the potential problems a user could face with withdrawing payments. When a user requests a withdrawal, they can take up to seven days to process the withdrawal. They say "This allows time to recall loans, should this be required". Again, this is a classic hallmark of a Ponzi scheme.

And finally, the last warning flag is the method they claim to use to generate these returns for investors. Their explanation of how they generate these high returns is incredibly vague and provides no detail. Its explanations also does not detail any risk involved. Again, the similarities between this and other Ponzi schemes are incredibly easy to see.

Another worrying aspect of companies like this is that not only are they obviously dangerous to investors who deposit their funds, expecting a high rate of return, they also provide loans on which they take double the loans value as collateral. To add to this again, they also operate as a cryptocurrency exchange. This means the capacity for schemes like this to rob people is huge. They will be able to rip off three different kinds of customers, not just savers. The Ponzi scheme is well and truly evolving for the 21st century and despite these incredibly obvious warning signs, these companies are continuing to grow and proliferate.

Cult-like cultures in crypto now

One of the biggest enablers of these modern day Ponzi schemes is the internet and the ease with which people can communicate and spread their ideas. Whilst this is obviously a great thing, the only issue is that the internet gives people the ability to be anonymous online and so the promotion of Ponzi schemes can happen more easily and with no consequences. It is much easier for investors to feel a part of something and much easier for people with nefarious motives to manipulate and trick people out of their money.

The likes of the GameStop saga have popularised gambling on stocks and cryptocurrencies with people in online forums encouraging people to buy assets that are currently being pumped. This online culture around cryptocurrencies is part of the appeal to investors. When investors buy cryptocurrencies, they are buying into a whole scene. They view themselves as radical or participating in counterculture which makes people think less about the risk involved or about the fact they are most likely being manipulated.

There are a few recent examples of well-known figures in the business world tweeting a message of support for a cryptocurrency which then makes investors pile in and drive the price up. Because these figures are often popular figures, people don't question their motives behind publicly promoting a cryptocurrency in this way. It only serves to pump the price up before it crashes and leaves all these investors at a loss.

A notable example of this was a U-turn by Tesla founder, Elon Musk who was a public supporter of Bitcoin and would often speak of its virtues. After publicly supporting the currency over a period of time and even allowing his company to accept Bitcoin as payment for his cars, he suddenly u-turned and said his company would no longer accept Bitcoin. He cited Bitcoins horrendous environmental impact as the reason for this. As a result, the price of Bitcoin crashed. Whilst this could have been a genuine change of heart when he was presented with new evidence, it could also be something more sinister. The point is, that the culture surrounding these cryptocurrencies makes it much easier for people to fall victim to Ponzi schemes.

Looking at the groups known Ponzi schemes like OneCoin used, you can see striking similarities between them and many cryptocurrency forums on the likes of Reddit or on popular messaging apps. In the case of OneCoin, people were trained to believe anyone that had a different opinion about the currency to them was wrong or that they were just "haters". This is really not much different to a lot of groups online today. If Charles Ponzi had had access to these resources in his time, you can safely assume his groups would look no different to the ones today.

Chapter 5:

How does it all end?

Answering the question of how the current mania and mass speculation around cryptocurrencies comes to an end is actually pretty simple. There are so many historical examples of Ponzi schemes and market bubbles to draw parallels from, a prediction of how the cryptocurrency mania comes to an end doesn't require a huge amount of speculation. There are a lot of similarities between the current cryptocurrency mania and the market bubbles that have come before. If we just look at crypto mania as a market bubble, we can make some predictions on what happens next.

There have been many notable market bubbles throughout recent history. They are surprisingly common throughout history and they all share similar hallmarks, most commonly excess speculation, greed, fear and exuberance. With the benefit of hindsight, each bubble is fairly obvious now looking back, but every time a new one happens, we all wonder how we didn't see it coming. The best way to try and spot new market bubbles is by looking back at previous ones and learning what happened and why.

The five stages of a market bubble

Historic market bubbles have been observed to all follow the same lifecycle. Hyman P. Minsky first defined the five stages that make up a market bubble in the 1980's in his book "Stabilising an unstable economy". The five stages he identified are:

1. Displacement. This occurs when something happens to create new paradigm such as a disruptive new technology or low interest rates.

2. Boom. Early on after a displacement, prices tend to rise relatively slowly as more and more investors enter the market. As word spreads, the asset starts getting a lot of attention and widespread media coverage. Fear of missing out sets in as investors pile in trying to get in before the ship sails. This fuels more speculation and draws even more investors.

3. Euphoria. During the euphoria stage, investors throw caution to the wind, seeing the market rising fast and thinking it can only keep going up. The greater fool theory plays its part during this phase as speculation is rampant. Investors create reasons and metrics to justify the new high prices.

4. Profit taking. During the profit taking stage, some of the early investors, the so called "smart money" start recognising the mania and the fact that a bubble exists. The bubble is about to burst, not knowing when this will happen exactly, they start cashing in positions and locking in profits.

5. **Panic.** The panic stage is when it all comes crashing down. It often doesn't need a huge event to tip things over the edge. It can be something small that starts a sell off and crash and once the crash starts, it crashes fast. Speculators facing margin calls, liquidate positions at any price, the supply vastly outweighs demand and prices tumble.

These five stages can be seen on the graph below showing the anatomy of a typical market bubble.

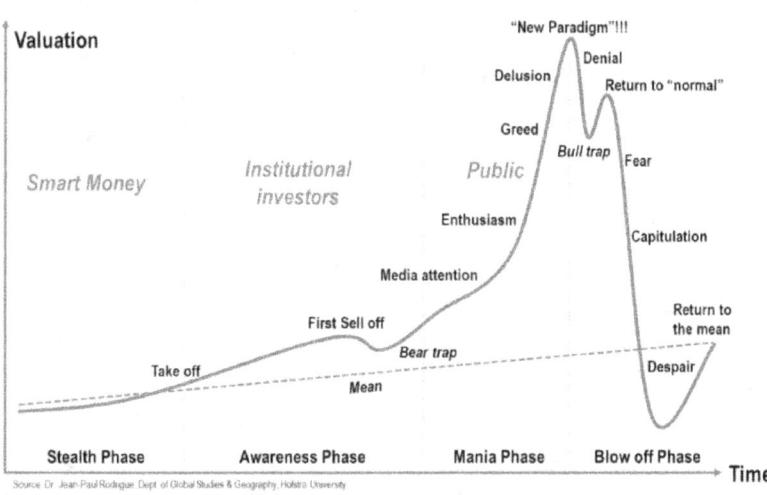

The psychology of market bubbles

There are several psychological phenomena that fuel market bubbles and allow them to become so devastating.

Chapter 5: How does it all end?

The psychological phenomena involved with speculative bubbles and Ponzi schemes are actually very similar.

The first is the herd behaviour of individuals in financial markets, also known as the bandwagon effect. Individuals act as part of a group, making decisions as a group that they would not make as individuals. Individuals also find it hard to believe that such a large group of people could be wrong and follow the mistaken belief that the group knows something the individual does not. They follow the analysis of the group and not their own. Finally, the social pressure to conform means people tend to act in the same way as a group, even if that act goes against an individual's natural instincts. This herd effect has a history of starting large, unfounded market rallies and sell offs that are often based on a lack of evidence or research to support either.

Another effect that comes into play is known as the hot hand fallacy or simply, over confidence. This is a behavioural bias where an individual believes they are less at risk of a negative outcome happening to them than the rest of the population. Essentially, this means the belief that whatever is happening now, will continue to happen forever. Investors and traders fall victim to this bias most often when they have made big profits in the past or observed others making big profits and therefore underestimate the probability of a downturn in markets in future. They often become too confident in their valuations and believe them too strongly, making them less likely to recognise mistakes in their valuations.

The final phenomenon that comes into play during financial bubbles is called prospect theory. This is the theory that states that as a market goes up, people become less risk averse and more willing to gamble, further fuelling rising asset prices. Part of this theory also states that investors also suffer from loss aversion where they are reluctant to sell when asset prices start falling as they are unwilling to crystallise a loss. This results in them holding onto investments for too long before eventually panic selling and fuelling a price crash.

Tulip mania of the 1630's

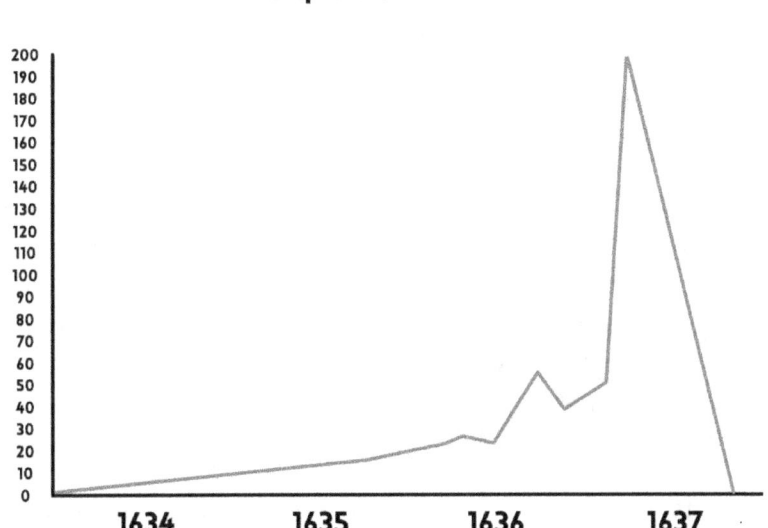

The earliest recorded major financial market bubble occurred in Holland in the 1630's and involved the trade of

Tulips. Tulips were first introduced to Europe from present day Turkey and became a status symbol in Dutch society. The Dutch at the time were world leaders in terms of their economic system. They were the first to create a stock market for example. The innovation that allowed the Tulip mania bubble to form was the introduction of what was essentially futures contracts system for Tulip bulbs.

In the Northern Hemisphere, Tulips bloom in April and May for one week. The plants could only be uprooted and moved about during the plants dormant phase between June and September. During these months, Tulip bulbs could be actively traded in the "spot market" meaning that if you bought a bulb, you could take delivery of it there and then. During the rest of the year, when the bulbs could not be uprooted and moved, tulip traders signed contracts before a notary to buy the bulbs at the end of the season when they could be uprooted and moved. This was in essence, a futures contract.

As the flowers grew in popularity across Europe, throughout the early 1630's, they became the fourth leading export of the Netherlands by 1636. The price of rare Tulip varieties that took years to selectively breed and cultivate rose initially throughout 1636 but towards the end of the year, the prices of common varieties started increasing.

The price of Tulips in the Winter of 1636 eventually skyrocketed as people speculated in the market, buying futures contracts without ever seeing the bulbs. Ordinary people were becoming rich over night when selling these contracts. At its peak, contracts were changing hands up to ten times a day. The greater fool theory fuelled this mass speculation and as often happens with market bubbles, a vast cross section of Dutch society got involved.

No deliveries of Tulip bulbs were ever made under these contracts as in February 1637, tulip prices crashed and the trade of the futures contracts came to a halt. The collapse began when buyers refused to show up at a routine tulip auction. An outbreak of bubonic plague may have been to blame for this at the time but this event was enough to dent confidence in the market. Tulip traders soon could no longer find buyers willing to pay inflated prices for their bulbs. As realisation set it, the bubble burst and many were left with contracts to purchase bulbs at prices ten times higher than that on the open market and others were left with bulbs worth just a fraction of what they paid for them.

Minsky's five stages of a market bubble are easy to spot in this case. Stage one, the displacement was both this new flower introduced to Europe, the Tulip that the wealthy sought as a status symbol and the innovation that was the futures contract. The boom stage is also easy to identify by the slow increase in popularity of the flower across Europe in the early 1630's. The Euphoria and profit taking stages occurred during late 1636 and early 1637. Finally, the panic stage in February 1637 when something as benign as a poorly attended auction, possibly related to the plague and not the tulip market, dented confidence in the market and sparked the crash that happened soon after.

Comparing the Tulip price index graph above with the typical speculative market bubble graph, you can also see the patterns are very similar.

Fast forward a few hundred years and the world experienced a recession so deep and prolonged, it became known as the great depression. The great depression started in America. A few years after the end of the First World War, America's economy was booming. The total wealth in the U.S more than doubled and GDP was growing at 4.7% per year. Breakthroughs in mass production made new technologies such as cars, radios and aviation accessible to the general public for the first time. Consumer debt soared where Americans were taking on debt to purchase these new goods that were widely available for the first time. These industries soon took off, fuelled by consumer credit and their share prices soared.

Seeing the opportunity, many started investing in the stock market. It became fashionable to "be in the market". Many people were taking up leveraged positions, buying shares on margin without fully realising the risks. It was common to be able to access leverage of 10 times where an investor could invest just 10% of a stock's price to make a stock purchase but not realising they would have to pay the full amount if the price fell.

Stock market speculation became rampant where investors were no longer researching good stocks to buy, they were buying anything in the belief that the market would just keep going up. Again the greater fool theory came into play here. Weak regulation allowed major financial institutions to join in with the mass speculation and the market kept rising.

The market could not keep rising forever. Experienced investors started recognising the situation in the Autumn of 1929 and the profit taking started. The mass production that had fuelled the boom, soon led to over production at many companies and farms that soon started having to sell their goods at a loss. The oversupply of both agricultural and industrial goods, causes prices to drop which decimated profits and began to hurt enterprises that were already laden with debt.

Profit taking combined with loss making businesses caused stock prices to stutter and starting on the 24th October, they finally crashed. This resulted in almost half of banks in the US collapsing, industrial production halved, and GDP dropped by 30%. By 1933, the unemployment rate in the US reached 24.9%. Many overleveraged investors had lost everything and many when they lost their jobs could no longer pay the debts they had racked up during the 20's. The collapse of the stock markets in the US sparked a worldwide recession that lasted throughout the 1930's.

The boom and bust of the 1920's and 30's also followed Minsky's five steps. The first stage, the displacement was the mass production that made many new technologies accessible to many for the first time. Prices rose modestly at first in the period immediately after the First World War and accelerated throughout the 1920's, marking stage two. Stage three was marked by the euphoria, mass leveraged speculation and massive consumer debt. The profit taking of the Autumn of 1929 marked stage four and the collapse starting on the 24th October marked stage five.

When you compare the Dow Jones Industrial Average graph above with the typical speculative market bubble graph, you can also see the similarities between them both.

Japans lost decade of 1980's and 1990's

Nikkei 225

In the 1970's and 80's Japans economy was booming. It was experiencing the fastest economic growth of any country in the world. The government eased regulation on the banking system, causing the money supply to increase and interest rates to fall. With record low interest rate and easy to access credit, many started to speculate in the financial markets.

Speculation became a core strategy for many Japanese corporations. It was easy for them to obtain money on the financial markets which they more often than not, recycled into further speculative market activities. As stock prices in Japan rose higher, fuelled by this speculation, the very companies that were speculating were able to report record profits. Investors then rushed to buy the stock of these companies, further inflating the bubble. It was estimated that at the end of the 1980's, about 50% of reported profits from Japanese companies came from these speculative investments. Because land in Japan commands a high price due to its scarcity, banks were accepting land as collateral for loans, causing land prices to skyrocket as well.

By 1989, the Japanese government was becoming increasingly concerned with these skyrocketing stock and land prices. In an effort to quell the speculation and reduce the supply of cheap money, the government raised interest rates seven times between May 1989 and August 1990. This caused stock prices to plummet at the start of 1990. Throughout the 1990's, Japan experienced slower growth than any other industrialised nation. This decade became known as "the lost decade" in Japan.

Minsky's five stages could be seen here too. Once again, record low interest rates marked the first stage. Stage two was marked by the early 1970's as the Japanese government loosened regulation on their financial system, causing an increase in the money supply and the start of a stock market bull run. The late 1980's marked stage three where speculation was rife and fiscal responsibility went out the window. Towards the end of 1989 marked stage four where the Japanese government recognised there was a problem and started to act in an effort to improve the situation. Stage five was market by the start of 1990 where stock prices crashed.

Look again at the similarities between the Nikkei 225 graph and the typical speculative market bubble graph. Again, the similarities are there.

Dot com bubble of the 1990's

Nasdaq Composite Index

During the 1990's, many believed traditional business cycles and recessions no longer applied and that booms were not necessarily followed by busts. The dot com bubble proved that theory wrong. It was started by the mass adoption of the internet. Throughout the 1990's, computers became cheaper and more widespread and advances in software made the World Wide Web accessible for millions.

The potential for the internet was clear and many technology start-ups started appearing on the market. Investors assumed that any company that operated online was going to be big. This speculation was helped in part by mass media coverage of these companies. Venture capital was easy for these companies to access and stock prices soon started to rise. Investment banks who were making record profits on Initial Public Offerings (IPO's) for these companies, fuelled speculation and encouraged further investment in technology. Investors started ignoring the fact that many of these companies were yet to make a profit, believing that they would eventually become profitable. Investors once again threw caution to the wind, not wanting to miss out on the opportunities that the internet brought. Prices continued to rise, companies that were not profitable were trading at disproportionately high prices. It was not uncommon to see stock prices triple or quadruple after an IPO.

The spending habits of a lot of these companies did not help the situation. Mottos such as "get large or get lost" were common and encouraged start-ups to invest heavily in marketing, often offering their services at a loss or even free. They believed that in future, they could then charge their customers more for their services once they had seen the value of them. Fiscal responsibility went out the window with many of these companies that had no proprietary technology, customers or products, essentially making them worthless. It was reported that some of these companies spent up to 90% of their budgets on advertising.

Once again, where fiscal irresponsibility and mass speculation are involved, things ended badly. The bubble burst. In March 2000, the threat of higher interest rates, news that Japan had entered another recession and rumours that big companies were dumping their shares were enough to spark a global stock sell off that disproportionately affected technology stocks. Throughout the rest of 2000 and 2001, many companies were forced to re-evaluate their spending habits just as investors were forced to re-evaluate theirs. Venture capital dried up and soon many companies folded as they had no services, intellectual property, customers or cash flow.

In the aftermath, millions of retail investors lost large sums of money. The chances are, you know someone that lost money in the dot com bubble. Some of the investment firms responsible for misleading investors such as Merrill Lynch and Citigroup were fined for their part.

The displacement that marked stage one of this market bubble was the internet, with stage two occurring in the early 90's as the internet slowly grew in popularity. Stage three was clearly marked in the late 90's when the internet had become widespread, venture capital was readily accessible and mass speculation was rampant. Stage four was marked with rumours that several leading companies such as Dell and Cisco were placing large sell orders their own shares. Finally, the crash in the months that followed marked stage five.

As with the other bubbles, the Nasdaq Composite Index graph shows similarities to the typical speculative market bubble graph.

Prior to the COVID-19 recession in 2020, the global financial crisis was considered as the most severe recession since the great depression. The roots of the global financial crisis actually lay in the bursting of the dot com bubble. In the aftermath of the dot com bubble, central banks and governments in the West lowered interest rates from around 6% in 2000 to around 1% by 2003. The aim of this was to increase the supply of money and encourage businesses and people to spend money and therefore boost growth and get western economies back on their feet after the dot com bubble burst.

In the US, mortgage rates were at a record low and they were incredibly easy to get hold of. Many Americans re-mortgaged homes or bought second homes. The spending spree fuelled by cheap credit allowed house prices to rise at record rates. The combination of record rises in house prices as well as cheap, easy to obtain credit fuelled speculation in the housing market. As with previous bubbles, the greater fool theory came into play again.

Banks were getting more and more irresponsible with their lending policies, giving people mortgages that would never be able to pay them back. These bad mortgages were known as "subprime" mortgages. It was estimated that the proportion of subprime mortgage debt in the US rose from historical lows of around 8% to over 20% between 2004 and 2006. To make matters worse, about 90% of these subprime mortgages had interest rates that rose over time. Banks bundled these up into packages known as collateralized debt obligations (CDO's), gave them favourable risk ratings and then sold them as investments all over the world.

Banks and investors all over the world were investing in these CDOs as they offered better returns than government securities and their favourable risk rating made them seem that they were also relatively low risk.

In mid-2006, house prices in the US peaked and soon began to stutter. As mortgage rates on subprime mortgages began to increase, mortgage delinquency rates started increasing. Demand for housing started to drop and along with it, house prices dropped. As house prices dropped, it became harder for people to refinance their adjustable rate mortgages, causing mortgage delinquency rates to further increase. This cycle continued and caused a crash in the housing market in the US.

As a result of exploding mortgage delinquency rates, the CDOs that banks all over the world had invested in, lost most of their value causing major liquidity issues in banks around the world. Many banks started failing and many started requesting government bailouts in order to survive. The fall in liquidity then caused a stock market crash as investors pulled out funds to try and keep their heads above the water. The result of all this was that by 2009, house prices in the US had dropped by 30% and the stock market by 50%. Some of the biggest banks in the world failed, others had to be bailed out with taxpayers' money and millions of people lost their jobs as the recession hit.

As with the other bubbles throughout history, Minsky's 5 stages could be observed. The first stage, the displacement was record low interest rates after the dot com crash. Stage two was around 2003 when these low interest rates started slowly driving up house prices. Stage three was between 2004 and 2006 when subprime mortgage debt increased to record levels. Stage four could be observed in 2006 when the market peaked and prices started to stutter and stage five was in 2007 when the markets crashed.

When comparing the S&P 500 graph above to the typical speculative market bubble graph, the peak isn't as severe but the common features of a large rise in a short period of time and a sharper drop after this are both there.

The crypto bubble 2020's

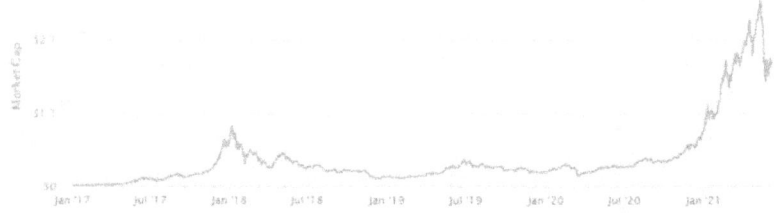

Cryptocurrency total market capitalisation

You can trace the roots of the current crypto bubble back to the global financial crisis in 2008. This crisis sparked a deep distrust of the banking system as many saw bankers as the cause of the crisis. The recklessness, corruption and greed of the banks involved in dubious sub-prime mortgage lending made many people want a better system, free of the corruption and greed of overpaid bankers.

This is why the first cryptocurrency, Bitcoin was invented in January 2009. As discussed in Chapter 2, Bitcoin was invented as a currency that would be free from any sort of central control and therefore be free from the corruption and greed of banks. Like many new technologies, the uptake of Bitcoin was slow at first but by 2013, it was catching on. Its price was slowly starting to rise. By 2013 however, Bitcoin was no longer the only cryptocurrency on the scene, there were now a total of 66 different cryptocurrencies. Over the next few years, cryptocurrencies grew in popularity, in 2017 there were now 1,335 cryptocurrencies.

Cryptocurrencies grew in popularity over the next few years, with thousand more coins popping up, each promising some new innovation that was going to change the world and become incredibly valuable. The total market cap of all cryptocurrencies hit a record high of around $750 billion USD in 2017 before pulling back to between $200 billion USD and $300 billion USD over the next few years. When the pandemic hit in early 2020, the market dipped to around $150 billion USD.

Around the world, lockdowns were imposed, severely limiting the ability of millions of businesses to trade. Governments acted to try and prevent the worst impacts of this. Interest rates were slashed to record lows to increase the money supply and vast support schemes to loan businesses money were set up in many countries. Interest rates in the USA were dropped to 0.25% and in the UK, 0.1%. In the USA, the government went a step further. Their $3.5 trillion USD support package included three rounds of stimulus pay-outs to every single American. These stimulus pay-outs in total were worth up to $3,200 USD per adult and up to $2,500 USD per child. These payments were intended to encourage Americans to spend money and keep their economy afloat. Needless to say, a lot of this money found its way into both the stock market and the cryptocurrency markets.

The global cryptocurrency market cap grew steadily throughout the rest of 2020 and exploded in 2021 to over $2.5 trillion USD in the middle of May 2021. This was fuelled by mass speculation, the proliferation of day trading gurus, euphoric online forums and of course as is often the case in market bubbles, an oversupply of cheap, and in the US, free money. Countless investors have thrown caution to the wind, buying into cryptocurrency without any research or due diligence. People are buying worthless assets that have no real world practical use or ability to generate any sort of cash flow. Word of mouth helps the markets reach new heights as many see the gains family and friends have made and don't want to miss out. Again, as we've seen, this often happens with both market bubbles and Ponzi schemes.

So can we see Minsky's five stages playing out here and if so, what stage are we at? I think you can see Minsky's five stages developing very clearly in this case. The dislocation that marked the first stage was the 2008 financial crash and the advent of the first cryptocurrency that came with it. The second stage can be observed clearly by the slow and steady rise of the total cryptocurrency market cap between 2008 and 2020. The euphoria of stage three is clear in between January and May 2021 when prices exploded and speculation was rife, driving the total cryptocurrency market cap to multiples of its previous record. Stage four is currently less clear. Towards the end of May 2021, the market started to stutter due to increased regulatory pressure in China. This could well mark the profit taking of stage four and signal that stage five is only around the corner.

If you also compare the cryptocurrency total market cap graph to the typical speculative bubble graph, the similarities are unmistakeable. It all points to a bubble that is yet to burst.

At the time of writing, this bubble has not yet burst. The brief drop towards the end of May 2021, caused by increased regulatory pressure in China signals that confidence in the cryptocurrency market may be more fragile than internet forums would have you believe. It was not a surprise that China intended to crack down on the proliferation of cryptocurrencies. Yet their announcement in May 2021 that banned financial institutions in China from offering any cryptocurrency related services seemed to come as a shock to the market. This might be an indication that many cryptocurrency investors, do not fully understand what they have invested in and leads to the possibility that a relatively minor unforeseen event could cause panic selling and pop the bubble that has formed.

Whilst it is uncertain exactly how and when this all plays out, it is clear that the bubble is there and that it will burst. A common theme in every market bubble in history has been the belief that it won't happen this time. This is not true, it will burst eventually, booms and busts are an inevitability of free markets.

For anyone reading that still strongly believes in the merits of cryptocurrencies and that the best thing to do is hold and hope for the best, think of the possibility that we are in stage four of a market bubble and that now might be your last chance to cash out before it all comes crashing down.

Closing thoughts

Underneath the bright lights and social media hype, we've seen how the world of cryptocurrencies isn't what it's portrayed to be by many. It is a shady world of Ponzi schemes to speculative bubbles, with con men everywhere ready to take money from naïve investors.

So should we avoid cryptocurrencies? Well we've seen that historically, speculative bubbles always burst and how mathematically, Ponzi schemes always fail. This leads to the conclusion that cryptocurrencies as they exist today will end the same way, they will eventually fail, becoming almost worthless.

This doesn't necessarily mean you shouldn't buy them, by all means buy cryptocurrencies as long as you understand the risk you are taking. Remember the likelihood that the cryptocurrency you are considering is simply a scam, pump and dump, Ponzi scheme or a purely speculative bubble. When buying cryptocurrencies, it is important to recognise that you aren't investing, you are speculating or gambling and could lose everything. Remember that even if the price is rising now, it is only a matter of time before it comes crashing down. Bear in mind that the people singing praises on social media and saying they are holding long term, are most likely manipulating you to drive the prices higher so they can profit. Remember not to get taken in by the promises of getting rich quick on cryptocurrencies that an endless number of snake oil salesmen are pedalling online.

With those points in mind, you're probably going to be better off avoiding them in the long run and at the very least taking profits if you are already invested.

If future mainstream currencies are going to be cryptocurrencies, they most certainly are not going to be any that you can buy on the market now. They will be cryptocurrencies that are created and regulated by central banks because without regulation and backing from central banks and governments, a currency cannot become widely adopted and useful. Whilst a distrust of central banks and governments is popular nowadays, the reality of the matter is that the centralised monetary system we have today is what has enabled the world to develop as it has. Regulations have evolved to avoid crashes like the 2008 financial crisis. Centralised monetary systems are a necessity in order to soften or avoid the worst economic crashes that have happened in the past.

Cryptocurrencies were originally invented to solve a problem that doesn't really exist. Cryptocurrencies don't give people back control, they actually remove the ability of economies to control their money supply and if they were widely adopted, would put the world at risk of much deeper and longer recessions and crashes in future.

The narratives surrounding their use case is constantly evolving to try and explain their ever rising prices. The rising prices and speculation cannot go on forever. As I've said, the bubble always bursts and the Ponzi scheme always fails. With the cryptocurrency market, it is only a matter of time before it all comes crashing down.

Other books by Alastair Dorsett

A fresh perspective on investing. In light of the recent turmoil in the stock market, the author has set out to arm new investors with the knowledge they need to cut through the noise and avoid common mistakes.

Available at all good online bookstores.

About the author

Alastair is a Chartered Engineer, he designs fighter jets by day and by night he is an avid investor and author. Part of his profession involves taking complex ideas and making them easy to understand. Engineers are trained how to meticulously research and apply logic. These principles are reflected in his books "What the F*ck Is Investing?" and "Cryptocurrencies: Ponzi Schemes, Bubbles and Bitcoin". With this book he saw an opportunity to make investing principles easier to understand for everyone and therefore make investing more accessible.

He grew up on the North Coast of Ireland before moving to England to study Aerospace Engineering. He now lives and works in England with his young family.

Connect with Alastair at www.wtfinvesting.com

If you found this book helpful, please leave a review so that more people can find this book.

www.ingramcontent.com/pod-product-compliance
Lightning Source LLC
Chambersburg PA
CBHW070416220526
45466CB00004B/1422